The Battle of
Towton

The Battle of
Towton

A.W. Boardman

SUTTON PUBLISHING

First published in 1994 by Alan Sutton Publishing Limited,
an imprint of Sutton Publishing Limited

This new edition first published in 2000 by Sutton Publishing Limited
Phoenix Mill · Thrupp · Stroud · Gloucestershire GL5 2BU

Copyright © A.W. Boardman, 1994, 2000

All rights reserved. No part of this publication may be reproduced, stored
in a retrieval system, or transmitted, in any form, or by any means,
electronic, mechanical, photocopying, recording or otherwise, without the
prior permission of the publisher and copyright holder.

A catalogue record for this book is available from the British Library

ISBN 0 7509 2479 9

Typeset in 10/13pt Bembo.
Typesetting and origination by
Sutton Publishing Limited.
Printed and bound in Great Britain by
Cox and Wyman, Reading, Berkshire.

Contents

Foreword

Battlefields have a profound fascination for us. As a member of the Battlefields Panel set up by English Heritage to advise the government about the conservation of battlefields and battle sites, I have been trying to analyse the causes of that fascination. Mainly it is because at a particular place and time masses of men met together to settle their argument 'à l'outrance', to put it to the test of death. They are places where great skill, great loyalty, great courage, great perfidy, great cowardice, great stupidity have been shown, where men have gone to their deaths because of passionate belief, uncontrollable rage, or in the control of a code and a discipline so powerful that it has seemed better to perish than to escape them. Whatever frightfulness has happened, whatever idiocy perpetrated, whatever glory achieved, it has been done in the most absolute fashion, even when the action was not in the long run decisive.

A battlefield is also a tomb, holding the bodies of most of those who died there, in Towton's case a very great number; a perpetual shrine and memorial which should engage our thought and our reverence.

To know what really happened – at Crécy, Agincourt, Poitiers, Patay, Castillon, Towton – that is the other fascination. It is impossible to reach the whole truth. Not even those who fought knew it all, but we can work towards the truth of the event. Known fact, reported fact, archaeological evidence, literary evidence and, under control, imagination are our guides. To that add a passion and a dedication to the understanding of the event and the terrain and the personalities involved and you may well glimpse truth.

It is a passion: when another says, or writes that one's own conclusions about the action of a battle are wrong, the response is fierce, and the re-examination intense. Andrew Boardman's account of Towton, one of the bloodiest and most raging battles of the medieval wars, is a marvel of evocation. He knows the history, which is extremely limited in particulars, and he has studied and discussed every possible clue. He knows the terrain both with exactitude and understanding and he has a fine regard for what that great battlefield historian Colonel Alfred Burne called 'Inherent Military Probability'. He is passionate in pursuit of the truth about this particular, this dreadful battle, and I believe that you will find in his vivid recounting of it more than fitful images of the grim truth about Towton Field, which lies today much unchanged since it lay in snow and blood on Palm Sunday 1461.

Robert Hardy, CBE, Hon.D.Lett.
Trustee of the Royal Armouries,
HM Tower of London
Consultant to the Mary Rose Trust, etc.

Preface

I do not recall the first time I visited Towton battlefield, but I do know that its fascination and interest have always been part of my life. The rolling, windswept plateau with its ingrained story of carnage and downright barbaric brutality is neither a morbid fascination on my part, nor, for that matter, a romantic one, and the riveting interest that attracts others to the story of the battle of Towton has, I have to say, become more and more incomprehensible to me over the years the closer I have researched it. True, as a battle, Towton is just one of a kind and could have taken place almost anywhere in Britain at any time or in any era, but, because we are dealing with an event in what have become known as the Wars of the Roses, the battle immediately takes on a different role for many and herein lies the 'hook'. The initial interest is suddenly fuelled, albeit incorrectly, with some other imagery that springs to mind, namely Laurence Olivier's emphatic portrayal of Shakespeare's Richard III: surrounded by his enemies at Bosworth; two warring factions picking red and white roses for emblems; princes murdered in the Tower of London and a kingdom continually raked by bloody and tragic civil war. This, I am sure, is the basic driving force behind some people's deep-down interest for this period in history, if they would only admit it, and also probably the first spark that has ultimately led many down the slippery slope from this into a total obsession with the subject in some cases, and into incomprehensible fascination in others.

However, the events leading up to the clash of Yorkist and Lancastrian armies between the villages of Towton and Saxton, in what is now North Yorkshire, is a far more complicated story to unravel and understand completely. As one leading author proclaims, quite rightly, 'acts have consequences in history', and the Wars of the Roses are no exception to this rule. In fact it is very dangerous to comment on the battle of Towton unless this is kept in mind due to its lack of written evidence. Indeed in my case this is where the fascination for the battle lies, it being a product of a long sequence of events. Such circumstances dictated why Towton was not only such a great and decisive military victory, but also such a great tragedy, played out to its utmost on fields that still bear the scars of its victims' graves.

The battle of Towton, like Bosworth in 1485, is also an important event in British history in that it placed a new dynasty on the English throne. This ultimately led to there being two anointed kings in England, each one contesting the other's right to rule. Later this situation caused further repercussions when the victor of Towton, Edward IV, finally rid himself of the problem. Ten years after Towton he murdered his opposite number, Henry VI, to secure the crown.

Coupled with these unusual and influential historical events is a more personal interest regarding why men go to war at all. Not only does the act of agression in battle seem to defy the laws of so-called civilized society, but it is quite simply very difficult for me to comprehend such a terrible and threatening situation without ever having been involved in a war. To further confound this understanding, while at the same time increasing the fascination, both of my grandfathers experienced the horror of two world wars, and one would not even talk about it.

With the subject of the battle of Towton we are faced with violence at its most basic level, and we may wonder at the kind of men that fought in it. It is easy to claim that medieval man was different in some way – perhaps given more to acts of brutality because of the type of world he was living in. But what of the pastoral farmer or the artisan, dragged away from his family and land, and marched hundreds of miles out of loyalty to an unfamiliar part of the country to do battle? What price these men's feelings of compassion or hatred when the arrows started to fly and the contending armies finally locked in mortal combat? Surely such 'conscripts' must have witnessed the same hellish sights on the battlefield and, after the event, suffered mental recoil similar to that experienced by some twentieth-century veterans. Therefore, with much deeper concepts to explore than immediately apparent, the fascination in the battle of Towton is very much hidden in the question of how this singularly bloody encounter ever occurred at all, and why soldiers took up arms against a foe who did not threaten their existence unless they bore arms also.

For the nobles, who were largely responsible for the Wars of the Roses, it was a far more protracted matter. As a result of the inevitable division between those who chose to take different sides in the conflict, local disputes became more polarized and land titles were an ongoing prize to slaughter each other for on the battlefield. This is where the blood feuds and personal 'vendettas' sprang from, as one nobleman became more powerful than another, or was continually favoured by the king while his counterpart was brushed aside and even, in some cases, murdered to get him out of the way.

All of these questions need to be explored because they were enacted out in some form during the battle of Towton, arguably the biggest, longest and bloodiest military engagement on British soil. I have never seen any constructive argument in stating categorically the number of men who fought in the battle, how many died on the battlefield and how long the fighting lasted. However, I do think it worthwhile to point out some of the conclusions I have reached after studying the battle for over fifteen years, based on other similar encounters and army arrays involved in the Wars of the Roses. So armed I can hazard an educated guess as to numbers. The arguments will undoubtedly go on, and who am I to say they should stop. After all, this fact alone has made the battle of Towton controversial, and rightly so. When the supposition is taken away and the disputes stop, the subject will, in my opinion, lose its interest.

The battlefield of Towton is a firm friend of mine, and I am fortunate indeed to have it lying, so to speak, in my own back yard. Over the years I have walked its ground in all weathers and have seen many changes, thankfully never affecting too much its timeless appeal for me. Consequently it is very depressing not only to hear of similar battlefields being threatened and destroyed by the march of twentieth-century development and industry, but also to visit areas that now show no signs of there ever being a battle site there. I do not understand how anyone in authority can condone such disregard for our heritage by constructing roads, quarries and housing estates across these very important landmarks.

I admit that conservation has never been such a high priority of my own, but if our stately homes are any indication of historical 'presence' then battlefields such as Towton are more so. It goes without saying that of Britain's major historical decisions, most of the important ones were made on battlefields, and if conservation through action is what it takes to protect these places, I am for conservation.

Acknowledgements

I would like to thank everyone who has helped me with the production of this book, in particular Robert Hardy CBE for his excellent foreword, advice and interest in the project, John Taylor of Leeds University, Victor H. Watson CBE, Hedley Marsden, Alain Brione, Chris Milnes and Denise Smith. I would also like to thank Michael Rayner of the Battlefields Trust, all at the Lance and Longbow Society, Graham Hudson, Phil Haigh, Martyn Cawood, Simon Richardson, Bob Thomas, Paul Barker, Andrew Green, David Hill of Castle Hill Farm, and last but not least, the staff of The Crooked Billet, The Greyhound and The Rockingham Arms public houses for their support over the years, and for providing the refreshments after my many explorations of the battlefield.

A big thank you is due to the staff of Leeds City Library and its local history section, the Yorkshire Archaeological Society, the Borthwick Institute, York, and all at Sutton Publishing for their help and advice. I am grateful to Random House UK Ltd for permission to reproduce the extract on pp. 4–5 from John Keegan, *The Face of Battle* (© John Keegan 1976, Random House UK Ltd (UK), Viking Penguin (US)).

I would like to give special thanks to my family and friends for their support. My father especially has been a battle of Towton enthusiast all his life; I owe my interest in all things medieval and military to him.

Andrew W. Boardman

ONE

'O miserable and luckless race!'

On 7 April 1461 George Neville, Bishop of Exeter and Chancellor of England, wrote to Francesco Coppini, the Papal Legate and Bishop of Terni, in Flanders, that on Palm Sunday:

there was a great conflict, which began with the rising of the sun, and lasted until the tenth hour of the night, so great was the pertinacity and boldness of the men, who never heeded the possibility of a miserable death. Of the enemy who fled, great numbers were drowned in the river near the town of Tadcaster, eight miles from York, because they themselves had broken the bridge to cut our passage that way, so that none could pass, and a great part of the rest who got away who gathered in the said town and city, were slain and so many dead bodies were seen as to cover an area six miles long by three broad and about four furlongs. In this battle eleven lords of the enemy fell, including the Earl of Devon, the Earl of Northumberland, Lord Clifford and Neville with some knights, and from what we hear from persons worthy of confidence, some 28,000 persons perished on one side and the other. O miserable and luckless race![1]

George Neville was writing of the battle of Towton, in which his brother Richard, the Earl of Warwick, had taken an active part. The document, preserved in the Calendars of State Papers of Milan, is evidence of what has become known as the longest, biggest and bloodiest killing field on British soil. In the same letter, Neville gives his own very personal opinion of the wars between the houses of York and Lancaster, known later as the Wars of the Roses. It smacks of the futility of civil strife in contrast with what he later points out might have been energies better directed 'against the enemies of the Christian name'.[2]

The bishop opened his letter by saying that he learned of these events from 'messengers and letters, as well as by popular report',[3] meaning, presumably, that his intelligence about the battle came directly from his brother Richard and King Edward IV, then in York, attempting to secure the area after their victory at Towton. Indeed, George Neville was commanded by Edward IV to join them in the north and help with this operation as soon as possible.

On 7 April Richard Beauchamp, Bishop of Salisbury, wrote to Coppini that:

> on Palm Sunday last King Edward began a very hard fought battle near York, in which the result remained doubtful the whole day, until at length victory declared itself on his side, at a moment when those present declared that almost all of our side despaired of it, so great was the strength and dash of our adversaries, had not the prince single-handed cast himself into the fray as he did so notably, with the greatest of human courage. . . . The heralds counted 28,000 slain, a number unheard of in our realm for almost a thousand years, without counting those wounded and drowned.[4]

The Bishop of Elpin, Nicholas O'Flanagan, added to Coppini's reports by stating that 28,000 were killed in the battle, 800 being on King Edward's side.[5] Another letter from London to a Milanese merchant, Pigello Portinaro, on 14 April, claimed that 28,000 fell, 8,000 of them being Yorkists.[6]

These correspondents communicate the earliest surviving 'newsworthy' reports of the battle of Towton in existence and, as such, their letters must rate very highly as containing unique facts about the battle from a mainly clerical viewpoint. However, we must remember that Coppini was hearing news from two pro-Yorkists claiming that the Lancastrians were the aggressors and that the 'late' King Henry VI was a 'puppet' in their hands. Indeed Coppini was pro-Yorkist himself. The other two letters seem diplomatically impartial, even though they may have received news from the same source. More important is that all of them communicate the atmosphere and feelings in London in the first weeks after the battle of Towton at a time when the anonymous author in the city claimed that 'I am unable to declare how well the commons love and adore him [Edward IV] as if he were their God' and that 'The entire kingdom keeps holiday for the event, which seems a boon from above'.[7]

The private letters of the Paston family of Norfolk also communicated Edward's victory at Towton, confirming the casualty figures given above. In this case William Paston reported to John:

You will be pleased to know the news my lady of York [Edward IV's mother] had in a letter of credence signed by our sovereign lord King Edward, which reached her safely today, Easter eve, at eleven o'clock, and was seen and read by me William Paston. First our sovereign lord has won the field, and on the monday after Palm Sunday he was received in York with great solemnity and processions. And the mayor and commons contrived to have his grace through Lord Montagu and Lord Berners, who, before the king came into the city, asked him for grace for the said city, which he granted them. On the king's side Lord Fitzwalter was killed, and Lord Scrope badly hurt. John Stafford and Horne of Kent are dead, and Humphrey Stafford and William Hastings made knights, among others Blount is knighted. On the other side Lord Clifford, Lord Neville, Lord Welles, Lord Willoughby, Anthony Lord Scales, Lord Harry and apparently the Earl of Northumberland, Andrew Trollope and many other gentlemen and commoners, to the number of 20,000, are dead.' [On a piece of paper attached to this letter, 28,000 dead were numbered by the heralds.][8]

So much for Yorkist correspondents. What of the Lancastrians, the main victims of the Towton battlefield slaughterhouse? What price their cause, and who reported for them, without bias, after the fateful day when the true anointed King Henry VI of England was ousted by the sword from his throne, his peers attained and their lands prey to the victor's greed? What drove the contending houses of York and Lancaster to such a 'great conflict', in which the unusually heavy casualties presented an accounting problem, both on and off the field, for the heralds, and resulted in rivers running red with blood and a rout that was mercilessly followed up into the night?

The State Papers of Milan and the Paston Letters tell only a small part of the story of the Wars of the Roses, and the dour dealings and dynastic struggle for power in the second half of the fifteenth century. The rest of the period's history is, of course, prized from the great, if sometimes inaccurate, chroniclers of Britain, not forgetting writers in Burgundy and France – equal players in the drama. Edward Hall, Polydore Vergil, John

Whethamstede, William Worcester, Philip de Commynes, Jean de Waurin and William Gregory – to name but a few – light a medieval candle in history with which we can see the all too obscure flickers of times past appearing, then disappearing at the crucial moment, leaving us in the all too familiar land of conjecture and supposition in which to seek the truth.

We must therefore put other sources to work to get nearer to the facts, and we must question the structure of historical events when eyewitness accounts are lacking. Even where 'firsthand' reports exist, one might argue, several accounts would need to be consulted to get a accurate perspective of the battle of Towton, for each man in battle may only have perceived his own immediate area of conflict. Lacking an overall aerial view of the battlefield, not to mention the danger a man might expose himself to if he took even a casual glance over his shoulder during such a fight, the soldier's story would be his own, which might prove tactically worthless when the battle was over. It is nevertheless important armed with available contemporary evidence of men in battle to illustrate the human experience of war and its consequences, something sadly omitted in the glory and heraldic pomp of some medieval battle historians' accounts.

Information on who was present at the battle of Towton and what motivated the combatants' actions on the day lie in attainder documents and the chronicles. The topography of the area must be evaluated to answer such questions as how terrain swayed the contending armies' movements and to what extent the land precipitated victory or defeat. Archaeology can be useful in locating graves and entrenchments, but, more important, finds may pinpoint personal regalia, which may be important in identifying whose troops were present. Logistics can answer such questions as what provoked manoeuvres before and during a battle, which troops were better equipped to survive the mêlée and, being thus armed, what disadvantages could overtake them when they ran. However, to conclude confidently why some men stood their ground and others fled, we must in the end evaluate the reasons for the armies being there in the first place, the effects of fatigue on morale and, of course, the human spirit.

John Keegan, the author of *The Face of Battle*, one of the half-dozen best books on warfare to appear in the English language, suggests that:

The answer to some of these questions must be highly conjectural, interesting though that conjecture might be. But to others, we can certainly offer answers which fall within a fairly narrow bracket of probability, because the parameters of the questions are technical. Where speed of movement, density of formations, effect of weapons, for example, are concerned, we can test our suppositions against the known defensive qualities of armour plate, penetrative power of arrows, dimensions and capacities of the human body, carrying power and speed of the horse. And from a reasonable assessment of probabilities about these military mechanics, we may be able to leap towards an understanding of the dynamics of the battle itself and the spirit of the armies which fought it.[9]

To answer our questions, however, we must begin much earlier than the battle of Towton, so as to clarify matters such as the commanders' motivations and the events leading up to Edward Plantagenet's seizure of the crown in 1461. It is therefore essential to be aware of the history of England from as far back as 1399 at least. From this date we may see the kindling of a feudal fire that burned – and was stoked with fuel more than once, then extinguished and reignited time and time again – until the Tudor age killed off the last of the Plantagenets and their pretenders to the throne, as much with the pen as with the sword.

The history of Britain and of the Wars of the Roses can be read in detail in many fine books on the subject. My intention here is to give the reader some of the facts that will be useful in understanding the events surrounding the battle of Towton. Without dwelling on irrelevant details, I hope to explain who was who, and why, through all of the politics, the wars became a dynastic issue tainted with the blood of revenge in 1461. To quote Shakespeare, my aim is 'to turn the accomplishment of many years into an hourglass'.[10]

The Origins of the Wars of the Roses

Henry Bolingbroke, Duke of Lancaster, usurped the English throne from Richard II in 1399. Later, when Henry sat on the throne and Richard was dead (probably murdered at Pontefract Castle), a new precedent, set in 1327, was again applied to threaten English kingship from then on. This precedent successfully unseated Edward II and meant that instead of a king ruling by lawful and legitimate right, he was more and more regarded as the

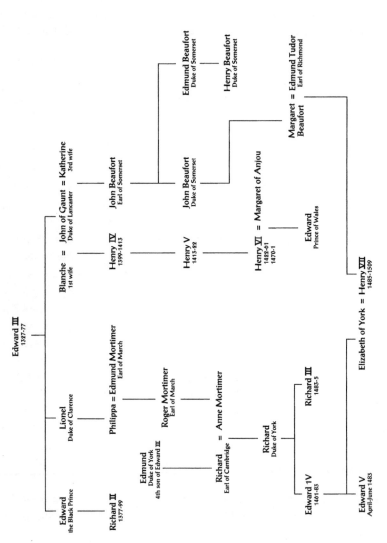

A simplified genealogical table of the contending houses of York and Lancaster

first among equals in the eyes of 'the princes of the blood'. Thus a serious loophole was left for a dissatisfied noble to exploit if the king was weak or lacked support. Henry Bolingbroke exploited this situation when Richard II seized his lands after the death of his father, the Duke of Lancaster, and matters escalated until his hands were finally on the throne of, in his eyes, an unfit king.

In becoming Henry IV, the first Lancastrian king, Bolingbroke also ignored another contender for the throne in Edmund Mortimer, whose father had been heir presumptive to Richard II but was never acknowledged as such by the then king. Henry was a strong monarch and the Mortimer claims to the throne were never pressed until, in 1415, others tried unsuccessfully. On the eve of Henry V's expedition to France, Richard, Earl of Cambridge, attempted to put his brother-in-law, Mortimer, on the throne. As a result he was executed for treason. The plot was uncovered and revealed to the king by none other than Mortimer himself, in an act of betrayal, thus putting the issue, and his brother-in-law, to rest for the time being.

Henry V, another strong king, sailed to Harfleur and marched into battle at Agincourt. Here the king's brother, Edward, Duke of York, died on the field, probably from a heart attack. His title passed to the late Earl of Cambridge's son, Richard Plantagenet, and thus the House of York was founded.

Henry V left his son a legacy of unfinished business in France. The trouble was that Henry VI of England and France was a nine-month-old child at the time of his father's untimely death from dysentery in 1422. To quote a political medieval cliche: 'Woe to thee, O land, when thy king is a child', but the Hundred Years War nevertheless thundered on in favour of the House of Lancaster, until at last, through lack of finance, the English were forced to fall back.

The king's French causes had been left in the hands of Henry V's brother, John, Duke of Bedford, but, when he died in 1435, two arguing factions emerged to contend whether the war should be continued, or whether peace through a treaty was the answer to the drain on the English war chest. On the one hand nobles such as Henry VI's uncle, Humphrey, Duke of Gloucester, the Lancastrian heir apparent, violently opposed a truce, while on the other side a party led by William de la Pole, later Duke of Suffolk, wished to negotiate with the French, and silence Gloucester in the process, for their own ends.

The Beaufort family, eventually Dukes of Somerset, sided with William de la Pole in an attempt to marry off Henry VI to a French princess. This eventually placed Margaret of Anjou, daughter of René, Count of Anjou, at the side of the king as Queen of England. Coupled with the Treaty of Tours, signed in 1444, this event precipitated the wane in the Duke of Gloucester's power and credibility, and contributed to the rise of William de la Pole and the Beauforts' authority at court.

From the personalities and events described so far we can claim that 1399 is an important year at which to begin to understand not the start of the Wars of the Roses, but the families, and their ties, who contended for position and power in them later. Some, like Henry VI, were born into a usurped throne and held the crown through 'right of conquest', not through 'right of descent', although, in fairness, Henry's grandfather, Bolingbroke, claimed the throne through his father, John of Gaunt, Duke of Lancaster, the third son of Edward III. Others, like Richard Plantagenet, Duke of York, could claim descent from Edward III's fourth son, through his father Richard, Earl of Cambridge, traitor to Henry V. Richard became Duke of York when his uncle Edward died at Agincourt in 1415, but this was not his only claim. On his mother's side, through the dormant Mortimer line, Richard was also descended from Lionel, Duke of Clarence, Edward III's second son.

Some nobles, such as the Beauforts, were equally placed to have a say in how England should be ruled, as they too had a claim to the throne, through John of Gaunt's third wife, Katherine Swynford. It should be argued here that the Beauforts' claims, if they ever surfaced, were somewhat tenuous. Nevertheless, when Edmund Beaufort became Duke of Somerset he became a court favourite and received appointments and power from Henry VI. Meanwhile Richard, Duke of York, received nothing but bad debts through his own financing of the war in France.

These three powerful men, plus the queen and the factious nobles supporting them, were to cause the wars between York and Lancaster.

To illustrate exactly when the Duke of York became suspicious of the Beauforts' directive hands behind King Henry's commands, we must look to 1447. In that year the enmity that the two factions had for each other surfaced when the lieutenancy of France was transferred from Richard, Duke of York, to Edmund, Duke of Somerset, then only an earl. The Duke of York was given the blame for the reversals in France and was appointed

King Henry's lieutenant in Ireland, obviously to get him out of the way of the Lancastrians' powerbroking activities in England. In 1447 Humphrey, Duke of Gloucester, was accused of treason, imprisoned and probably poisoned to death by agents of the Duke of Suffolk, Somerset's ally. Soon afterwards Suffolk himself was murdered for similar crimes. With Gloucester's death the Duke of York became heir apparent, and even at this early stage he must have been wondering who would be the next to pay for what was clearly Somerset's ambitious nature. Suffolk, it seems, became the victim of his own high-powered intrigue. As for Somerset and his new-found appointment in France, when the English were defeated at Formigny in Normandy, he dared not return to England and sought refuge in Calais until the storm clouds blew over.

A few weeks later, in the summer of 1450, Jack Cade's rebellion highlighted the fact that reform was in the hearts and minds of many people, to the extent that London was for a time in anarchy. The rebels who entered the city were men of Kent and, as such, their grievances, although common feelings, were vented violently on some of the king's chief councillors, in particular those who had offended their county. In the midst of the riots, hundreds of people were killed and murdered in the city, and the rebellion was only finally put down when Cade was eventually caught and executed. However, the questions about the king and his advisers' capabilities did not go away.

With so much trouble at home it is not surprising that the Duke of Somerset chose to return to England from Calais to protect his own position. The Duke of York also stirred himself from Ireland, as insinuations were already being made that he had been responsible for Cade's rebellion. After all, York had been favoured in the 'commons' manifesto and Somerset branded as one of 'certain persons who daily and nightly are about the king's person and daily inform him that good is evil and evil is good'.[11]

The heated encounter between the two dukes in London was disastrous and occurred against the backcloth of thousands of armed retainers bullying each other for position. It was clear to York that favour was still being bestowed by the king, and increasingly the queen, Margaret of Anjou, on his rival Somerset, despite his attempts to sway the king in the guise of being a true subject and champion of law and order. Disgruntled, but firm in his resolve, York decided to canvass support from the Duke of Norfolk and the

Earl of Devon, who were the only prominent nobles willing to go along with his open criticism of the court. Somerset by this time had been given the captaincy of the Calais garrison, the king's fickle but professional standing army abroad, and his military failure in France was soon forgotten. This appointment gave Somerset the edge again in his political battle against the Duke of York, which in the end forced York over the precipice as, diplomatically, he had failed miserably.

Somerset and York's intentions were now clear, in so much as both were protecting their own political lives, there being no evidence at this time that either of them were coveting the throne. Henry VI, removed from the feud in mind if not in body, watched the squabbling dukes with increasing tension, seemingly unable to comprehend either the gravity of the situation or the possible outcome of such a rift. Obviously he did not think either noble was capable or wanted to dethrone him in a similar fashion to the usurpation of 1399, otherwise he may have acted against such a threat immediately. Even taking into account his numbness to events, Queen Margaret, who was to become a dominant influence in the wars later, certainly favoured Somerset and did not suspect him of greater ambitions. However, from her point of view at least, the Duke of York was another matter entirely.

The queen's gradual understanding of her husband's shortcomings, maritally as well as politically displeasing, made her suspect York, as heir to the throne, of being a typical over-mighty subject, bent on a course of ultimate power, and a threatening catalyst, by which her own position and plans might be consumed. She misjudged the situation badly because England was not like France, fraught with generations of factional intrigue and war, although periodically it was to become so by her refuelling of the situation through nobles who were sympathetic to her cause.

Escalating matters, in February 1452 the Duke of York marched on London from his castle at Ludlow to enforce Somerset's downfall. He encountered the royal army at Dartford and quickly occupied a strong defensive position, which he fortified with guns. York proceeded to make his position clear, declaring that he wished the king no harm but that 'he would have the Duke of Somerset, or else he would die therefore'.[12] However, as time passed, and under increasing pressure from the king's emissaries to avoid 'the effusion of Christian blood', a meeting was arranged where the Duke of York might present his grievances in person to the king.

Unfortunately York was tricked, and, after being escorted to London, he was forced into a humiliating upbraiding in front of his fellow peers. Somerset was vindicated of all charges raised against him while, at St Paul's in London, York was forced to make a public oath never again to disturb the peace. He returned to his castle at Ludlow a bitter man.

It is interesting to note that in the king's company at Dartford there were nobles, such as the Nevilles, who were to become staunch Yorkists only a few years later. This illustrates not only the effect of the king's mismanagement of the great magnates of the realm, but also that the polarization in England, caused by the quarrels between York and Somerset, was increasingly providing a convenient arena in which to settle local and ancient dynastic issues at the point of a sword. The Nevilles and the Percys offer classic examples of such behaviour, coming to blows across ever-shifting borders in the north of England, occasionally involving thousands of armed retainers in their feuds. Both families saw distinct advantages in being on opposite sides in the sporadic to-ing and fro-ing of the Wars of the Roses.

By 1453 the Nevilles, specifically the two Richards, the Earl of Salisbury and his son, the Earl of Warwick, were to be found siding with the Duke of York, as they too had come up against Somerset and the king in a dispute over land. The king succeeded once again in putting leading nobles at each other's throats instead of defusing the situation as his predecessors might have done. However, things became worse for King Henry because, on his way to attempt to dislodge Warwick from Cardiff Castle, he received news of a catastrophe in France. John Talbot, Earl of Shrewsbury, had been killed and his army routed at Castillon, and with this defeat all lands won in the Hundred Years War were lost. Only Calais remained English. Even worse, on receipt of news of the calamity, King Henry suffered a total mental breakdown, which reduced him to no better than a vegetable, unable to speak, hear, or understand his actions or what was going on around him. This, of course, left the kingdom effectively leaderless and eventually caused the Royal Council to meet with the Duke of York to discuss the situation, York still being, in theory at least, next in line to the throne.

If the Duke of York was looking to pull off a *coup d'état*, then, with the magnates who now supported his cause, this was the moment when he might have staked his claim to the throne and usurped it. However, York remained loyal to King Henry and was content to let the council imprison his enemy, Somerset, in the Tower of London.

Later a more legitimate obstacle emerged to bring the Duke of York once more down to earth. Queen Margaret gave birth to a son – an heir, who would give Somerset and York equal status once more and eventually give the Lancastrian cause added zeal and credibility. Of course, now the legitimacy of the child was to become the main focus of Yorkist attention, as in some circles the Duke of Somerset was named as the father, possibly giving rise to insinuations that this provoked the king's madness, the duke's ascendancy at court and the machinations of the queen. The implications concerning the king's pious and monk-like abhorrence of anything remotely sexual, and his depressive unwillingness to recognize the child when he was born, furthered these rumours considerably. Propaganda aside, it was nevertheless thought imperative, as the king's illness became well known, that the Duke of York should be made Protector as the north was once again becoming a battleground of Neville–Percy brawling.

The duke accepted the post 'grudgingly', we are told, but acted with venom, stripping Somerset of his captaincy of Calais, seating his friends in positions of power and quelling the northern dispute. The wheel of fortune was, however, about to turn full circle once again, because at Christmas 1454 the king recovered his sanity, removed Somerset from the Tower and reversed all of York's decisions. He also blessed his son, declaring that 'he never knew him until that time, nor what had been said to him, nor where he had been whilst he had been sick until now'.[13] By April 1455 the Yorkists were up in arms and on the march after the Duke of Somerset's blood. The scene was set for the first battle of St Albans.

The Wars 1455–60

Some historians have regarded the battle of St Albans as a mere 'scuffle in the streets', however, with approximately 5,000 men on the field in such a confined area, it can hardly have resembled a scuffle. Any armed incursion involving the king, and the leading nobles of the land with banners displayed in rebellion, must warrant the title of 'battle', however few the casualties might have been.

The Duke of York with his Neville supporters – Salisbury and Warwick – made camp at Key Field to the east of St Albans, while the king's army, under the command of the Duke of Buckingham, occupied the town. Mediators were again despatched to avoid battle, and also to accuse the

Duke of York of treason in answer to his scathing remarks about Somerset. However, this time, in difference to the Dartford affair, the talks broke down and an attack was launched by the Yorkists on the barriers of the town, which had hastily been fortified by Lord Clifford.

The main assault failed, but 600 of the Earl of Warwick's troops under Sir Robert Ogle found a gap in the defences and they burst into the town 'through garden sides between the sign of the Key and the sign of the Chequer',[14] two of the town's ancient inns. The Yorkists proceeded to roll up the Lancastrian defenders' flank, then shot hundreds of arrows into the resulting confused mass. The king's standard wavered and was left abandoned in the main street, many of his men were routed, and the residue, finding themselves hemmed in, sought refuge and cover in the buildings that lined St Albans market-place. Finally, finding the barricades weakened, more and more Yorkists pushed into St Peter's Street and the end of the fighting was signalled when the Duke of Somerset, the Earl of Northumberland, Lord Clifford and others were butchered to death in the last throes of Lancastrian defiance. The king, wounded and shocked, his horror of bloodshed a well-known characteristic, was conveniently bundled into St Alban's Abbey before the executions commenced. It was no accident that the nobles marked for death were the Duke of York and the Nevilles' greatest enemies in their quest for political supremacy .

The battle of St Albans signalled not only the start of the Wars of the Roses, but, more important, the unfurling of a bloody flag of revenge by the sons of the Lancastrian nobles killed there, who vowed to have the heads of the Yorkist lords thereafter. All three prominent nobles slain at St Albans had their namesakes at Towton in 1461, of whom young Lord John Clifford, whose father had commanded the defences at St Albans, was to become probably the most brave, able and subsequently vindictive one of them all.

After the engagement, York and his followers were absolved of all blame for the battle. Once again the duke grovelled and renewed his oath of allegiance to King Henry, which, if nothing else, highlights his fear of the king's sanctity, his sovereign's legitimate right to rule and his apparent acceptance of the Prince of Wales as heir to the throne. Also, now that Somerset was out of the way, York seemed content to right the wrongs in the land through his king, even from this new powerful political platform, and not to depose Henry for his weakness. As discussed earlier, he certainly had the opportunity to take the throne on several occasions in the early days of the Wars of the Roses.

The next year saw the reinstatement of the Duke of York as Protector, due to the king's continuing instability and his failure to quell disturbances in south-west England. With his subsequent dismissal from office in 1456, York once again found himself in a very dangerous situation, and it became increasingly obvious to him that the queen was now ruling both king and country with a firm hand. Queen Margaret, taking advantage of the absence of the Duke of York and his Neville allies in Scotland and Calais, began to consolidate her own position and that of those who supported her cause, in an effort to refuel aggression and bring about the Duke of York's demise. To this end she ordered that a large quantity of cannon should be removed from London to Kenilworth Castle, and by the close of 1456 the king and his court had moved to Leicester, with most offices recently held by Yorkists filled by Lancastrians. However, the slide towards the next bout of the wars was gradual, almost as if no one except the queen really wanted to continue hostilities.

Conscious attempts to reconcile the two parties occurred in 1458 in the public charade known as Love Day, during which each faction walked arm in arm to St Paul's. This event was more than likely instigated by the king, and had the effect of again bringing thousands of armed retainers to the city, almost igniting the political powder-keg there and then and achieving nothing but further mistrust on both sides.

In May 1458 the Earl of Warwick was resorting to piracy. He had been appointed captain of the Calais garrison on Somerset's death and was predictably being squeezed by the Lancastrians, receiving less and less money from the Exchequer to pay the troops under his command. When, out of necessity, he attacked the Hanseatic Bay fleet, he was summoned to London to explain his actions before the queen, who demanded his arrest. Warwick escaped back to Calais, claiming that there had been a plot to murder him. Because of these reversals and threats against them it is not surprising that the Yorkists were conspicuous by their absence when, in June 1459, a Great Council met at Coventry where York and the Nevilles were indicted for their failure to attend the king.

Apart from the military and political defeats they had suffered since the battle of St Albans in 1455, the Lancastrians were now once again controlling events. Sensing this advantage, every attempt was made to mobilize their forces to act while the Yorkist lords were widely scattered. At the same time the Duke of York made immediate plans to assemble his followers at Ludlow, sending messages to the Earl of Salisbury, in the north at Middleham Castle, and the Earl of Warwick, across the English Channel at Calais, to come to his aid. There is evidence, however, that York got wind of Lancastrian preparations for war and the possibility of a Lancastrian 'trap' in the Midlands much earlier, because the Act of Attainder passed on the leading Yorkists later in the year claimed that he had planned another coup against the king. The Duke of York, according to this evidence, may then have changed his attitude to King Henry's right to rule at this time. He may also have been reviewing his own political position in the light of the new pressures brought about by the queen, prompting him to act and to pre-empt a possible Lancastrian move against him at Coventry.

The two Neville earls, on receiving word of this new turn of events, prepared to march through gathering Lancastrian forces. Warwick, with men from the Calais garrison in his ranks, narrowly missed Somerset's contingents and reached Ludlow unscathed. However, his father, the Earl of Salisbury, was not so fortunate and was blocked by Lord Audley's army between Newcastle-under-Lyme and Market Drayton at Blore Heath. Here Salisbury ran into Lancastrian troops hoping to link up with the main armies of the king and queen nearby. Indeed the Lancastrians had failed badly in concentrating their forces, considering that the king's army was within ten miles of Blore Heath battlefield at the time of the action. The problems of concentration were also not helped by Lord Stanley who, always the cautious player, sent only fair promises to attend his majesty, echoes of a later confrontation with his sovereign Richard III at Bosworth in 1485. At Blore Heath, Stanley did not even turn up to fight, so Lord Audley faced the Yorkists alone.

By all accounts, when battle commenced the Lancastrians had the edge in numbers. However, they failed to shake the Yorkists from their elevated position in a battle line that is reputed to have withstood two cavalry charges and one infantry attack across a river and open terrain. Even though we have only meagre accounts of the battle from chronicles, are we to believe that cavalry attacks were even contemplated by Audley and his captains, who were surely well aware what longbows *en masse* were capable of doing to horsemen? Alternatively, Salisbury's small force may have been deficient of archers, as the Lancastrians may have been at St Albans, which could have provoked a bold decision by Audley to charge the Yorkists down. In anticipation of attack, Salisbury secured one of his flanks with a wagon laager and succeeded in beating off the repeated Lancastrian assaults. Finally, however, possibly leading one of these fateful cavalry charges uphill, or maybe the infantry assault when these failed, Audley was killed, unable to break the Yorkist line. Mounted medieval knights were certainly not the order of the day in England during the Wars of the Roses.

As already stressed, the wars between York and Lancaster were not lucky in their chroniclers, so historiography is not as simple as we would like. The tactical aspects concerning the battle of Blore Heath typically illustrate the disparity of chronicles, which is such a feature of the Wars of the Roses. The Towton story-line shares this problem, as it too lacks concrete facts about the battle from the pens of early historians. William Gregory, writing some ten years after the battle of Blore Heath, and Jean de Waurin had both had military experience, indeed Gregory was a soldier in the wars, yet neither of their accounts of the battle can be trusted to the letter. The culmination of this frustrating lack of contemporary evidence is best summed up by the attitude of one author writing a history of England in that he would not include details of the battles of the Wars of the Roses in his manuscript because of the doubtfulness of the available material.

Even though the Earl of Salisbury had driven Audley's force from the field, his own contingents were still in great danger because of the close proximity of the main Lancastrian army. His retreat is reported to have been covered by a Friar Austin, who 'shot guns all that night' to confuse the king's army.[15] Even though the majority of the Yorkists made good their escape, Salisbury's young sons were captured and imprisoned during the chase, highlighting the relentless pursuit of the unblooded Lancastrian army and its firm resolve to rectify the embarrassing situation it had created. The Earl of Salisbury crossed the River Severn in the face of the king's banner and headed for Ludlow. Here, once united, the Yorkists despatched letters to the king explaining their actions, but by now these petitions of innocence were becoming less believable and therefore falling on hollow ground.

Among the professional troops that Warwick had brought to Ludlow from Calais, the Master Porter, Andrew Trollope of Durham, was, in my opinion, to become the most influential military brain to affect the battles of the Wars of the Roses up to the events at Towton. His later exploits and partnership with the Duke of Somerset are somewhat of a prodigy in that eventually, as the duke's lieutenant, it is he who must be credited with changing the face of English warfare through tactical advantage and surprise during this period. This is something that his predecessors had failed to grasp fully. At Ludford Bridge, Trollope, with the Yorkists, drew his troops up behind their defences of guns, carts and stakes in an effort to defy the king. It was this act of defiance that forced Trollope into a difficult choice of loyalty and, in the end, into a dramatic decision that lost the Yorkists a crucial advantage in their struggle to keep their already morale-battered army in the field.

A rumour spread in the Duke of York's camp that the king had issued pardons to those who would not bear arms against him, and his forces arrayed for battle with banners displayed. This hearsay, whether or not true, certainly had the desired effect because Trollope, coming to England under the pretext that he would neither have to fight his sovereign nor commit treason, took his men and deserted to the Lancastrians during the night. What has become known as the rout of Ludford then took place – an event that was to plague Trollope for the rest of his short life, branding him a traitor in Yorkist eyes and later placing a price on his head, dead or alive.

When the decision was taken to quit the field the alarm was sounded at Ludford, and the Duke of York with his two sons, Edmund, Earl of Rutland, and Edward, Earl of March (later Edward IV of Towton fame), accompanied by Warwick and Salisbury, fled from their routing army via the quickest escape route into Wales, breaking bridges down to slow the pursuing Lancastrians. In the event, however, the Lancastrian army, now disbanded, were busy looting and pillaging Ludlow on one of the few occasions when troops violated a township and its people. The Duke of York took ship to Ireland, where he had been well liked as a lieutenant in previous years, and he and his son Edmund resided here until September 1460. Salisbury, Warwick and Edward fled to Calais. Subsequently, all of the Yorkists were attained by the king for their treasonable actions at Ludford, their estates were confiscated and their heirs disinherited.

It seemed that the Yorkist cause was in ruins. However, it was not to be the Duke of York, but the three earls who now took centre stage in the next scene of the drama. During the next few months, Warwick was to take the first steps on the road to what he considered his own political destiny and towards the grand title of 'Kingmaker', which history would label him with.

As will be seen later, the title is somewhat dubious given that his so-called understudies had their own ideas about where the crown should sit.

Strategically, Calais, the Yorkist earls' refuge, was a crucial tactical position of strength in that the Lancastrians could not afford to ignore its commercial, political and military significance. The English had held the port and outlying districts for over a hundred years since Edward III's reign. Given its position at the crossroads of northern Europe for trade in wool, not to mention its close proximity to France and Burgundy, the value here of a permanently manned garrison of 2,000 men was obvious. The Yorkist occupation therefore not only threatened the Lancastrians commercially, but also, indirectly, an alliance with Burgundy, for instance, might prove disastrous, just when Queen Margaret and her supporters had at last gained the upper hand through the king. In response to this threat, therefore, the new Duke of Somerset, Henry Beaufort, was duly appointed captain of Calais, and was despatched to recapture the port and remove the threat, which was growing stronger by the day in favour of the Yorkist earls.

However, the Lancastrian preparations had not been good and Somerset and his men, including Lord Roos, young Lord Audley and Andrew Trollope, were at once repulsed. They later had to resort to a series of 'guerrilla' actions against the Yorkists after securing the castle of Guines as a base for their operations. Meanwhile the Earl of Warwick had also not been wholly on the defensive, and in January 1460 Sir John Dinham raided Sandwich, successfully attacking a Lancastrian Calais-bound strike force led by Lord Rivers, thus thwarting another desperate plan to recapture the vital port. On the opposite side of the English Channel, Somerset kept up his harassing tactics as best he could under the circumstances, but his hands were tied in so much as he could not afford to keep up the payments due to his men. Warwick took full advantage of this lull in the battle for Calais and sailed for Ireland to confer with the Duke of York.

It is not known what took place, or what was discussed between the duke and earl in the two months preceding Warwick's return to Calais. The obvious must have been stated, of course, namely that an invasion of England must be attempted to secure their reinstatement to office, but what was this to involve? We can only guess at what necessary steps were conceived to prevent such attainders ever occurring again. The crown and its rightful head must have been on the agenda, one would have imagined, and Warwick for one may have even pushed for the Duke of York's eventual usurpation 'by his title of hereditary right',[16] purely out of his own lust for power at the expense of someone else's exposure to danger. However, by the end of their private conference, plans were laid for an invasion of England, and the Earl of Warwick set sail back to Calais.

On 26 June 1460 the Yorkists embarked for England with a few thousand men, but not before their way had been paved by a well executed propaganda campaign in Kent. A vital bridgehead had also been secured for them by the energetic Dinham, who this time captured Sandwich with the help of Sir John Wenlock and Warwick's uncle, Lord Fauconberg. Against all the odds and with the Papal Legate, Francesco Coppini, in their company, to give weight to their enterprise, Canterbury was reached without opposition. Here Sir John Scott of Ashford and the notorious Kentish captain, Robert Horne, joined their ever-increasing numbers. Originally the two men had been sent by the Lancastrians to do exactly the opposite and prevent the Yorkists from reaching the town, but the recruiting drive towards London continued and the old ally of the Duke of York, Lord Cobham, was also welcomed into the fold as the main Yorkist objective came within striking distance at last.

King Henry, then at Coventry, got word of the Yorkist invasion, but not before the earls had entered London unopposed, and bottled up the Tower garrison under Lords Scales and Hungerford with what was left of Lancastrian support. Because of this it was apparent that the king had to move south to counter the Yorkist invasion quickly, and it was equally important that the Yorkists should move to the attack before the Lancastrians could muster their full power.

The success of the earls' invasion in 1460 gives more credence to planning and vigorous action rather than luck. However, some of the Yorkist strikes at the south coast must have been very risky, to say the least, as the English Channel would have placed an unpredictable factor in the way of sound tactical planning. The commanders of the expeditionary assaults on Sandwich and its eventual capitulation must be given the medals here though, even if Warwick and the Duke of York had formulated the overall plan of action in Ireland. Also, inadvertently, some kind of Yorkist *esprit de corps* had been created in Calais, and, with the help of the Earl of Warwick, the youthful Edward, Earl of March, had gained confidence in his own abilities free from the restrictions placed on him by his father, the Duke of York. Consequently he attracted great respect and also recognized the abilities in the senior commanders who had led and carried out the successes of the invasion of 1460. The same men would eventually lead some of his contingents into battle at Towton the following year.

Propaganda must be given the credit for the means of invasion, and, as with some other important strategic gains in the Wars of the Roses, this element of political subterfuge alone by the Yorkists gained them 'footmen' and support from the main counties of Kent, Surrey and Sussex, which allowed their invasion plans to succeed.

Not everything went the Yorkists' way, however, because, before departing from London, the nobles had to reaffirm their earlier oaths that they wished not to harm the king but, echoing previous loyalties, that they had instead come to deliver him from his enemies. To this end various bishops, including Coppini, who was turning more and more Yorkist every day, were sent with the army to see that these oaths were kept. This had the effect of, on the one hand, gaining apparent religious approval for their actions and, on the other, the Yorkists having to put up with the interfering nuisance this might cause when military action was finally contemplated. All of this was brought about by the Yorkists' own earlier propaganda campaign to appeal to the people, the same people who were now accidentally being bombarded from the Tower by Lancastrians firing on Yorkist positions left in the command of the Earl of Salisbury, while Warwick, Edward and Fauconberg marched out of the city to find the king.

Leaving his wife and son at Coventry, the king advanced to Northampton and fortified a camp just outside the town on the banks of the River Nene between the river and Delapré Abbey. Here he endeavoured to muster more men to the royal banner, and, with the support of the Duke of Buckingham and Lords Grey, Beaumont and Egremont, he awaited the Yorkist challenge. The battle of Northampton saw the last time in the Wars of the Roses when a major attempt to avert bloodshed, through mediators and heralds, was made. The failure of the lofty prelates of the realm, who tried to negotiate a settlement, including no less than the Archbishop of Canterbury, not to mention the Pope's Legate, shows just how far the nobles were prepared to go in their quest for supremacy and the control of the king. The battle of Northampton was also the first time that Warwick, March and Fauconberg, the battle commanders at Towton, saw joint action. However, it was not the abilities of the Yorkist leaders that won the day this time: again luck and, more important, treachery were to help them to victory, and at the same time bring to the Wars of the Roses commander a new fear to contain within his army for time to come.

Resolute and confident in their fortified position, the Lancastrians despatched a last defiant message back to the Yorkists and took their positions behind their guns. Lord Grey of Ruthin was given the charge of the Lancastrian vaward (vanguard), traditionally the right or front battle of the army, and the Yorkists advanced to the attack. However, the Lancastrian artillery, thought to have been operational, had succumbed to damp in the waterlogged entrenchments and would not fire. This disaster allowed the Yorkist army time to scramble up the slippery embankments of the Lancastrian defensive earthwork. An even worse misfortune for the royal army was to follow. In what could have been a very bloody and costly assault by the Yorkists, the tide turned when Lord Grey and his men changed sides and, as one chronicler recorded, actually aided the struggling Yorkists over the redoubt into the camp. Once inside, with the help of Grey's men, the Lancastrian army crumbled. Buckingham, Beaumont and Egremont were cut down defending the king at his tent, while the remaining Lancastrians were routed, many drowning as they tried to escape across the River Nene.

It is certain a prearranged plan was executed at the battle of Northampton between Lord Grey and the Yorkists, possibly in accordance with feelings of genuine disloyalty on the part of the vaward commander. The evidence to support this is overwhelming, considering that a frontal foot assault on the strong Lancastrian position would have been, to say the least, foolhardy. At the ill-fated battle of Castillon in France, John Talbot was rendered almost unrecognizable by injuries when his English army attempted a similar assault against gun emplacements. In fact his herald only identified him after the battle by the characteristic gap in his teeth.

After Northampton, the king once more fell into Yorkist hands, and, on their triumphant return to London, Lord Scales and the defenders of the Tower capitulated. Some were executed on Warwick's orders. Consequently, when news of this defeat and the king's capture reached Somerset and Trollope, still defiantly in possession of Guines near Calais, they gave up also, and after handing the castle over to the Yorkists in return for their freedom they fled to France.

All now awaited the return of the Duke of York from Ireland, but even the staunchest Yorkists were unprepared for the next act that the noble Plantagenet was about to spring on them so rashly. Certainly Warwick for one was not pleased with the way York dived headlong into a very embarrassing scene in Westminster Palace on his return to London. John Whethamstede takes up the story:

And when he arrived there, he advanced with determined step until he reached the royal throne, and there he laid his hand on the cushion or bolster, like a man about to take possession of his right, and he kept his hand there for a short time. At last, drawing it back, he turned his face towards the people, and standing still under the cloth of state, he looked attentively at the gazing assembly. And while he stood there, looking down at the people, and awaiting their applause, Master Thomas Bouchier, the Archbishop of Canterbury, came up and after a suitable greeting, asked him whether he wished to come and see the lord king. At this request the Duke seemed to be irritated, and replied curtly in this way: 'I know of no person in this realm whom it does not behove to come to me and see my person, rather than that I should go and visit him.'[17]

In this vivid account the Duke of York seems to have 'died', in the very best theatrical sense, in front of the highest in the land, but nevertheless he was indeed claiming the throne. He then put forward his title through his ancestor Lionel, Duke of Clarence, the second son of Edward III, as opposed to King Henry's right through Edward III's third son, John of Gaunt. But after being unable to get any response to this either, he stormed out of the assembly, burst the bolts of the king's private apartments in a fit of rage and resided there for some time, brooding over his failure.

Everyone was absolutely dismayed, and the questions the Duke of York had raised were put before the lords, who claimed that such a matter was beyond their learning. In turn the problem was passed on to the judges, who were equally baffled, in that it was beyond the law to say who should or should not rule England. Eventually, however, a compromise was reached and the so-called Act of Accord called for Henry's right to rule, as he was the anointed king, but thereafter the Duke of York and his heirs were to succeed him. The Earl of Warwick and his brother, the Bishop of Exeter, George Neville, were involved in the settlement, as one might expect, and consequently there existed bad feelings between Warwick and York thereafter, possibly because the duke did not follow Warwick's plans discussed during their meeting in Ireland. Certainly there were angry words between them both, which may have turned the Earl of Warwick's head in the direction of Edward, Earl of March, to fulfil his own powerbroking machinations instead, as Edward, being the Duke of York's eldest son, was now second in line to the throne. The Lancastrians were equally vexed with the Duke of York's dynastic advances, especially the queen, for where did the new arrangements leave her son, the Prince of Wales, now that York was heir to the throne? Unlike the king, though, who it seems agreed to the settlement, the queen was not prepared to let this indignity occur without a fight. From her new base in Hull she set about gathering a large army to crush the Duke of York once and for all, reinstate King Henry and, more important, secure her son's inheritance.

The motivations of the two warring factions by the end of 1460 were now changed somewhat in that of the people who primarily caused the wars between York and Lancaster events had changed dramatically their present positions of power. The king was even more under the thumb of those who controlled him, and the queen, in assuming this domineering role, was, along with the young prince, now more a focus of Lancastrian hopes and strength. The old Duke of Somerset's sword had been picked up at St Albans by his more able son, who was to carry the bloody flag of revenge against the Yorkists thereafter. The Duke of York, probably lacking credibility and, now in his fifties, divested of some of his earlier gusto and sound judgement, had ended up, because of his respect for the crown of England, a victim of his own weakness. In the end this forced his hand to do the unthinkable and imitate Henry Bolingbroke's usurpation of 1399, emerging from his theatrical blunder a bruised, unstable and bitter man. Although still commanding respect from the house he had founded, many others may now have looked to his son Edward to fulfil the Yorkist dream under the guidance of Warwick the Kingmaker. The war, because of these events, had also undergone a significant change. It had turned from a quarrel between two men who sought control of the king for financial and political reasons into a dynastic issue and a battle for the right to wear the crown. However, the very same war was now about to undergo a further metamorphosis and to become, in some ways, a war between the north and south of England.

As an illustration of Queen Margaret's resolve to get even with the Yorkists for their attacks on the crown and her son, she sailed to Scotland, after conferring with her supporters in Hull, and there consulted Mary of Guelders and the young James III. The Scots promised her arms and men, on condition that the Prince of Wales would then be married to one of James's sisters and that the important garrison town of Berwick-upon-Tweed would be handed over to them. Harsh terms were suddenly replaced by unbelievably good news for the Lancastrians in the shape of a Yorkist disaster at Wakefield.

TWO

'Yet it rotteth not, nor shall it perish'

I n December 1460 Lancastrian movements in the north and Wales
caused the Duke of York to assemble his forces, in particular to come
to the aid of his Yorkshire tenants, who were being harassed by
the queen's troops. He despatched his eighteen-year-old son, Edward, Earl
of March, to collect support in the western marches. Then, after
gathering approximately 5,000 men and 'a great ordinance of guns and
other stuffs of war'[1] from the Tower of London, he set off north with his
younger son, Edmund, and the Earl of Salisbury to stamp out
the disturbances. His first disaster was hitting bad weather, and because his
artillery train could not cope with the rain and muddy roads it had to
be turned back. Then on reaching Worksop he came upon the vaward of
his army cut to pieces by an unknown enemy, which prompted him to
head for Sandal Castle near Wakefield, of which he was both lord and
owner. It was here that he, and many of his followers, spent their last
Christmas.

It is certain that this tactic of harassment was a Lancastrian ploy to
lure the duke into mainly staunch Lancastrian territory, but the skirmish
at Worksop may have been a pure chance encounter with forces
commanded by the Duke of Somerset and the Earl of Devon, marching
from the west country to join the assembling forces of the queen. Indeed
the array of Lancastrian peers that had gathered at Hull and later at
Pontefract Castle in opposition to the Duke of York's meagre army
was considerable, as it included the Dukes of Somerset and Exeter, Earls
of Devon and Northumberland, possibly the Earl of Wiltshire, numerous
other powerful lords such as Clifford, Roos, Neville, Dacre, and Andrew
Trollope. Their combined contingents are said to have numbered 15,000
men, a vast army by the standards of the day. Because of this threat
it was now quite clear that the Duke of York was isolated and cut off from
his allies. Without the help of Warwick, who was guarding London,
and Edward, far away in Shrewsbury, the duke had all too easily walked

into an untenable situation, which in the end would force him to commit a series of military and logistical blunders in the face of the enemy.

Under the promise of a truce between the two armies that would last until after Epiphany, York received Lord Neville at Sandal Castle. Davies' Chronicle relates what could happen in the Wars of the Roses when Commissions of Array were granted to unscrupulous nobles:

> Then the Lord Neville, brother to the Earl of Westmorland [a Lancastrian branch of the family] under a false colour went to the said Duke of York, desiring a commission of him for to raise a people for to chastise the rebels of the country, and the Duke it granted, deeming he had been true on his part. When he had his commission he raised to the number of 8,000 men, and brought them to the lords of the country, that is to say, the Earl of Northumberland, Lord Clifford and the Duke of Somerset, that were adversaries and enemies to Duke Richard.[2]

It is reasonable to assume that, because he had been doublecrossed by Neville, York was by this time an angry and desperate man. To make matters worse the Christmas festivities had probably taken their toll on the food available to his army. To keep even a small force in the field during times of plenty was always a problem in the fifteenth century, and living off the land, especially in one's own district, was not considered the best thing for public relations because, after all, this was the pool for levying troops. It was this lack of food and supplies that forced the Yorkists to take advantage of the brief respite in military operations, in accordance with the truce, to try to rectify their situation. William Worcester gave the basic details, if not the correct date, when the Duke of York made the fatal decision that would eventually lead to the imminent disaster at Wakefield and his death in battle:

> On the 29th day of the month of December at Wakefield, while the Duke of York's people were wandering about the district in search of victuals, a horrible battle was fought between the Duke of Somerset, the Earl of Northumberland and Lord Neville with a great army, and the other party, where there fell on the field the Duke of York, Thomas Neville, son of the Earl of Salisbury, Thomas Harrington and also many other knights and squires, and 2,000 of the common people.[3]

The battle of Wakefield had been brought about by the Duke of York's failing to grasp the situation he had fallen into; that his enemies were no longer prepared to keep faith with him, (the truce had been broken by the Lancastrians) and all through December 1460 he had continually committed a cardinal military sin – the underestimation of the enemy. Although the battle was over in a very short time, due to superb planning by the Lancastrians, its real story can sadly never be fully told because many chroniclers failed to understand why the Duke of York left the protective walls of Sandal Castle to encounter a vastly superior Lancastrian army in the fields below. However, Andrew Trollope seems to have been the brains behind the lure and successful ambush that followed. One reason suggested for the Duke of York's rash advance is that Trollope had dressed 400 of his men in Warwick's livery in the guise of reinforcements, in order to lower the duke's guard. This may be true, but would this have been sufficient to bring the duke's whole force out of the castle to greet them? It is more probable that a Lancastrian army of equal strength to the Yorkists presented itself before the castle the day after the foraging party, mentioned by Worcester, had been attacked, and thereby blockaded York's supply line to Wakefield. One imagines that this would have been irritating enough to force the Yorkists' hand to reopen the communication line to the town by force of arms. This action would have called for all of York's troops, then presumably stationed in and around the castle. (In the English Civil War, Sandal Castle could only garrison a small contingent of men in cramped conditions.)

The fact that even this reasonable manoeuvre was frowned on by veterans in York's army is highlighted by Sir David Hall's cautionary words before the engagement. The Tudor chronicler Edward Hall, Sir David's grandson, explains what happened next:

> The Duke of York with his people, descended down the hill in good order and array and was suffered to pass forward, towards the [Lancastrian] main battle, but when he was in the plain ground between his castle and the town of Wakefield he was environed on every side, like a fish in a net, or a deer in a buckstall, so that manfully fighting, was within half an hour slain and dead.[4]

Here then is the cause for the Yorkist defeat: an ambush executed by two Lancastrian forces emerging suddenly from woods on either side of what was then Wakefield Green or 'Pugneys', while the main force was fully engaged and drawing the Yorkists farther and farther away from the castle. A modern ploy, attributed to Andrew Trollope, carried off with precision by Lancastrians who were no longer prepared to keep faith with the Duke of York, nor, for that matter, with the accepted codes of chivalry.

If we are to believe what is said about where York fell in the battle (a small triangular piece of land marked by three ancient willow trees in hollow boggy ground, according to *A tour through the whole island of Great Britain* by Daniel Defoe, 1724–6), it seems probable that the duke was struck down almost immediately, as the main battlefield graves are to be found near to Portobello House, close to the River Calder. Human remains, swords and bits of armour were unearthed here in 1825, placing the end of the battle and the rout some way towards Wakefield. A back-edged sword, the forerunner of the more modern sabre blade, was found on this site and sold at Christies in 1966.

Attempting to escape the field, many chose to flee to the town, including the Duke of York's seventeen-year-old son, Edmund, Earl of Rutland, who crossed Wakefield Bridge in panic, with Lord Clifford in hot pursuit. Clifford, renowned as a kind of Lancastrian avenging angel, soon made short work of his prey, killing him in cold blood. Consequently Rutland was later pictured in some accounts as a pathetic little boy who was murdered as he tried to gain access to a house in the town, 'a little above the barrs beyond the bridge'.[5] Clifford is also supposed to have stabbed him in the presence of Rutland's tutor. His tutor was probably his tutor in arms, however, and, what is more, the young earl had more than likely made short work of some of his Lancastrian counterparts in the battle in an effort to make good his escape, which sheds a different light on the whole episode. William Gregory described Rutland as, 'one of the best disposed lords in this land',[6] and consequently his apparent murder by Clifford was later to stir Yorkist avenging angels to perform similar acts of execution in their turn.

Worse Lancastrian recriminations were yet to follow, and, as the heralds and gravediggers got to work at Wakefield, the Yorkist prisoners taken after the battle brooded over their fate behind Pontefract Castle's infamous walls. The Earl of Salisbury, who had been captured by a servant of Trollope's, was to have been ransomed for his life, but it was said that the common people who bore him a grudge took him by violence out of the prison and cut off his head. His death was also said to have been the work of the Bastard of Exeter.[7]

Other prisoners, including John Harrow, a Yorkist captain of foot, shared a similar fate at the block and the Yorkist nobles' bodies were interred at Pontefract. Salisbury, Rutland and the Duke of York's decapitated heads were removed to York, where they were spiked by the Lancastrians on Micklegate Bar. The Duke of York's head was adorned with a derisory paper crown, a fitting epitaph to a man whose every move had been dogged with frustration by his king's inability to rule the land well, his own lack of success in usurping the crown because of his respect for traditional loyalty and his later failure to judge the situation to make an effective change. The Duke of York's title and hereditary right, however, was not so easily severed from its trunk, and, as he had once claimed when making his stand in Parliament on his return from Ireland, his royal blood was perpetual and 'for though right for a time rest and be put to silence, yet it rotteth not, nor shall it perish'.[8] Edward, Earl of March, now Duke of York, was about to take his father's words and claim quite literally.

The Yorkist defeat at Wakefield left the Lancastrians drunk with success, even more so when Queen Margaret arrived with additional troops from the north, and now that the London road was open, final victory seemed to be only a matter of time and occasion. The superior tactical expertise shown at the battle of Wakefield, and the resulting extermination of the Duke of York, members of his family and some of the more valued Yorkist commanders, gave the Lancastrians new hope in the midst of almost continuous defeat in the field. Since 1455 the royal army had suffered no less than three major defeats, not to mention the battle for the control of Calais in 1460. Only the non-battle of Ludford can be credited to them. It therefore seems probable, because of this sudden turnaround at Wakefield, that the northern command now relied more on the professional talents of Andrew Trollope in military matters. Certainly Jean de Waurin, the Burgundian chronicler, rated Trollope's competence very highly above the nobles, and it is therefore equally likely that it was he who masterminded the Lancastrians' strike south in a midwinter campaign that would eventually sweep the Yorkists into disarray and retreat.

After Wakefield, a concerted plan of action was put into operation that involved both the victorious northern army of the queen and another pro-Lancastrian army commanded by Jasper Tudor and the Earl of Wiltshire. It is recorded that the Earl of Wiltshire landed in southern Wales with a force of Bretons, French and Irishmen, and united with Tudor in the hope of joining forces with the main Lancastrians marching on London. However, if Wiltshire fought at Wakefield on 30 December 1460, how did he manage to accomplish such a voyage – which must have been very difficult in winter down the North Sea coast and through the English Channel, picking up mercenaries on the way – and arrive in Wales at Pembroke on 20 January? This would have been a feat in those days, to say the least. The earl, however, is something of an elusive character, renowned especially for his feats of battlefield escapism. Considering his escape from the battle of St Albans in a monk's habit, along with his disappearance from two other major engagements, including Towton, we must leave his 'Grand Tour' of 1460 in the realms of pure conjecture for the moment. However, some sort of communication from the north to the Welsh Lancastrian army must have been employed, and the foreign mercenaries are authentic, so it may have been that Wiltshire rode across country to Pembroke after the battle of Wakefield and met the mercenary troops on the coast in response to a much wider pre-arranged plan. The fact that Wiltshire was at the battle of Wakefield is also a debatable subject, by the way.

Meanwhile at Shrewsbury, Edward, Earl of March, learned of the deaths of his father and brother. He was now the new Duke of York and also, according to the Act of Accord, the heir to the throne. Young Edward's state of mind at this time is illustrated by the speed at which he moved to the attack, first towards the perpetrators of his family's killings, then tempering this anger with a swift about turn when news reached him of the Welsh Lancastrians marching on Hereford. His castle at Wigmore provided the ideal look-out post as it protected one of the main routes into England and the marcher lands of his ancestors the Mortimers. Here and at Hereford nearby he gathered contingents on his own ground, many of whom would fight for him at Towton, and then awaited his enemies, contemplating what must have been uppermost in his mind at the time: revenge.

Edward was probably the most able commander of his day. His later exploits show his skill in timing, speed of recruiting and moving large armies great distances in adverse conditions. He did not lack courage either, fighting all of his battles on foot 'in the English manner', and always at the head of his contingents in the thick of the battle. However, like his counterparts the Lancastrians, he recognized the abilities of the 'great captains' in his army, using their knowledge to good effect, while at the same time making it obvious who was in charge. Many authors have belittled Edward's ability on the field of battle and in contrast highlighted the generalship and experience of such men as Warwick and his uncle, the old campaigner Lord Fauconberg. However, before and after the battle of Towton, Edward consistently showed his prowess as a commander and copybook medieval warrior. In contrast the Earl of Warwick was to fail miserably in battle, and later, when he had been thoroughly beaten and killed at Barnet in 1471 by his protégé, Edward was to conduct the most gruelling and frustrating campaign of the Wars of the Roses, in the Cotswolds, without him, culminating in the battle of Tewkesbury. Fauconberg, on the other hand, did not live long enough to participate in either battle. He died in 1464 and, his being Warwick's uncle, we can only speculate whose side he would have taken at Barnet when the chips were down.

The nobles in the Duke of York's company at Wigmore were therefore to fight against the advancing Lancastrians without the presence in their ranks of such large figures as Warwick and Fauconberg. This was a daunting test of credibility for an eighteen-year-old to overcome in the presence of doughty marcher lords who were entrusting their lands and estates to his care. In their eyes his limited military experience may have been questioned as well.

The Battle of Mortimers Cross

Various dates have been given for the battle of Mortimers Cross in 1461. The 1st, 2nd and 3rd of February are all possible days for a battle that is shrouded, like so many others, in legend through lack of historical evidence. William Worcester had this to say:

> On the vigil of the Purification of the Blessed Virgin [1 February 1461] a battle was fought near Wigmore at Mortimers Cross, when the Earl of March advanced with 51,000 men, [a gross exaggeration], against the Earl of Pembroke with 8,000, and from the field fled the Earl of Pembroke, the Earl of Wiltshire and many others.[9]

Gregory recorded that 'Also Edward, Earl of March, the Duke of York's son and heir had a great victory at Mortimers Cross in Wales the 2nd day of

February next following'.[10] Edward Hall, writing some time after the event, agreed with Gregory's Chronicle, the date being recorded as 'Candlemas Day in the morning',[11] 2 February, whereas recent research concerning the battle suggests 3 February, the feast day of St Blaise. The first week in the month will be good enough for our purposes. If we want to be really critical, the year was still 1460, as the new year in the fifteenth century started on 25 March. In fact the battle of Towton was only just fought in 1461 – such are the problems of dating medieval events.

Edward's army moved to the attack against the Earl of Wiltshire and Pembroke's motley force at the junction of four main routes on the banks of the River Lugg. It must have been a cold, crisp morning with a weak, wintry sun in the sky because, as the two forces arrayed for battle, a strange phenomenon was witnessed by Edward's army. William Gregory gave a brief description of the event in his chronicle, but Edward Hall expanded on the story he heard in saying that the Duke of York

> Met with his enemies in a fair plain, near to Mortimers Cross, not far from Hereford East, on Candlemas Day in the morning, at which time the sun, as some write, appeared to the Earl of March like three suns, and suddenly joined all together in one.[12]

Gregory plainly said, 'over him [Edward] men saw three suns shining',[13] giving rise not only to a legend but also to religious and heraldic symbolism. After the battle, Edward used this 'sun in splendour' as one of his livery badges. More important was that, on the day, the suns were allegedly changed by Edward's quick thinking from a portent of medieval doomsday into religious veneration. In explaining the first recorded parhelion (ice crystals refracting in the atmosphere) as the Father, Son and Holy Ghost, who were conveniently on the Yorkist side, Edward raised the morale of his awestruck troops. Sadly, however, we have no such clear, if somewhat fanciful, details of the battle itself or of the opposing armies' manoeuvres on the day.

Some accounts of Mortimers Cross state that, during the fighting, one Lancastrian 'battle' (division), thinking it had done enough, sat down while others engaged the enemy. At first glance this seems a little far-fetched given the Yorkist advantage in numbers. However, the lie of the land may point to not so incredible an event in that the Lancastrians may only have been able to bring part of their army to bear on such a narrow front. Indeed the present monument, at Kingsland, some distance from the crossroads, marks the southern edge of a narrow strip of land, running between the hills in the west and the River Lugg in the east. It may be safe to assume that the battle was fought somewhere in the vicinity, possibly with the river securing the flanks of both armies and the hills the other, Edward having his back to Mortimers Cross. Equally plausible, therefore, is the assumption that, because the Yorkist army was somewhat larger in this confined area, some of Edward's contingents may not have engaged either, but sat down like the Lancastrians, conserving energy behind the lines until they were ordered up. Gregory graphically depicted what happened when the Lancastrians broke and were routed under increasing pressure from the Yorkists, and what vengeance Edward wreaked on his enemies:

And there he took and slew knights and squires and others to the number of 3,000. And in that conflict Owen Tudor was taken and brought to Haverford-West [Hereford] and he was beheaded at the market place, and his head was set on the highest pinnacle of the market cross, and a mad woman combed his hair, and washed away the blood off his face, and got candles, and set about him burning more than a hundred. This Owen Tudor was father to the Earl of Pembroke and had married Queen Katherine, mother to King Henry VI. He thought and trusted all along that he would not be beheaded until he saw the axe and block, and when he was in his doublet he trusted on pardon and grace until the collar of his red velvet doublet was ripped off.... Then he said 'That head shall lie on the stock that was want to lie on Queen Katherine's lap', and put his heart and mind wholly on God, and very meekly took his death.[14]

Other Lancastrian captains were also executed, and thus Edward decisively disposed of the first threat to the House of York in ruthless fashion, although Pembroke and Wiltshire, undoubtedly his two main targets, made good their escape to fight another day. However, it must be said in fairness that, no matter how ruthless and vengeful Edward was at this time, it was neither this factor, nor the legend of the three suns, that won him the battle of Mortimers Cross. The Yorkist quality of command and soldiers under that command must be regarded as superior to the

Lancastrian forces. Men like Sir Walter Devereux, Lord Fitzwalter and Sir William Hastings were later to become Edward's right-hand men, and the quality of their retainers and the companies they recruited, not to mention the fact that they fought on ground of their own choosing, must have weighed heavily against the mixture of mercenaries and Welsh squires opposing them. The battle of Mortimers Cross was a decisive victory as well as a personal success and confidence drive for Edward, Duke of York. The west was secure, but Warwick in the east was yet to be tested.

Thirteen days after the battle of Wakefield, the unruly contingents under the command of Lord Neville pillaged the Yorkshire town of Beverley, setting the tone for the Lancastrian army's advance south, its ferocious reputation running before it, and causing fear and panic up and down the country. Many of 'the northerners' who plundered their way towards London were Scots, brought by Queen Margaret and allegedly promised by her that all lands south of the River Trent were fair game in lieu of wages. By giving these soldiers a free hand, the queen had inadvertently set wheels in motion that she would later be unable to control, even though the plundering troops may have been in the minority. The Prior of Croyland Abbey was among the most fearful of the Lancastrian 'chevauchée' (a term used to indicate an armed ride, involving pillage and looting) and wrote, almost reminiscent of Viking invasions, about defensive measures around his abbey:

The Northmen swept onwards like a whirlwind from the north and in their fury attempted to over-run the whole of England. Also at that time paupers and beggars flocked forth in infinite numbers, just like so many mice rushing forth from their holes, and abandoned themselves to plunder and rapine without regard to place or person. What do you suppose must have been our fears dwelling here in this island [Croyland Abbey] when every day rumours of this sad nature were reaching our ears, and we were in the utmost dread that we should experience similar hardships to those which had been inflicted by them upon our neighbours? In the meantime, at each gate of the monastery, and in the village adjoining, both at the rivers as well as on dry land watch was continually kept, and all the waters of the streams and weirs that surrounded the village, by means of which a passage might possibly be made, were rendered impassable by stakes and palisades of exceeding strength, so much so, that those within could on no account go forth without given leave first, nor yet could those without in any way effect an entrance. For really we were in straits, when word came to us that this army, so execrable and so abominable, had approached to within six miles of our boundaries. But blessed be God, who did not give us for a prey unto their teeth![15]

Croyland Abbey, along with many other religious houses, had much to protect in the way of wealth from the advancing Lancastrian 'whirlwind from the north', so much so that some of the wealthier, well-connected prelates paid professional soldiers protection money. The Bishop of Ely, for instance, hired thirty-five Burgundian mercenaries to guard his cathedral when news reached him that towns like Grantham, Stamford, Peterborough and Royston had already been looted by the queen's army. Luton fell to the ravages next, and by 16 February the defenders of Dunstable, captained by a local butcher, according to Gregory, were also beaten out of the town. Taking all this unruly behaviour into account we may safely assume that, by this time, the Lancastrian army was severely depleted. Most of the northerners would probably have deserted with their plunder, so the massive force that had driven south with such speed may by now have resembled the size of the army mustered before the battle of Wakefield, with a few of the more loyal Scottish troops still trying to keep their bargain with the queen.

The Second Battle of St Albans

The Earl of Warwick had by this time at last moved lethargically to the attack, but only after cautious defence measures had been put into play first. These measures were, in the end, to prove useless, chiefly because the Yorkist propaganda, which included scaremongering, backfired. In fact, fear of the 'northerners' before they reached London made many wavering midland and southern lords join the Lancastrians instead of alienating them. In the face of a victorious, powerful and pillaging army, this was a lot easier option than trying to defend land in the Wars of the Roses. Eventually, however, the Duke of Norfolk, dragging King Henry with him, moved out of London on 12 February, linking up with Warwick on the outskirts of St Albans just before the Lancastrians attacked Dunstable. William Gregory, who was probably in the Yorkist army and therefore an eyewitness, recounted in his chronicle the dithering, not to mention indecisiveness, of Warwick's command when news was received of the Lancastrian approach to the town:

> The lords in King Henry's party [the Yorkists in this case] pitched a field and fortified it very strongly, and like unwise men broke their array and field and took another, and before they were prepared for battle the queen's party was at hand with them in the town of St Albans, and then everything was to seek and out of order, for the scouts came not back to them to bring tidings how near the queen was, save one who came and said that she was 9 miles away.[16]

It seems from the evidence above that Warwick, unsure of the Lancastrian line of march to the town, had not received good intelligence from his 'scourers' (scouts). Consequently his battle array, most probably stretching like a dashed line from the Great Cross in the middle of St Albans over Barnet Heath and Nomansland Common to the eastern end of the town, had to be hastily moved when news arrived of an attack up the Dunstable road. Equally galling for Warwick's troops was the fact that this crucial realignment involved moving the fortifications that they had set up to redress the inequality that existed between themselves and the Lancastrian army. This was a long drawn-out manoeuvre, to say the least.

Abbot Whethamstede, who probably watched the second battle of St Albans from the abbey tower, continued the story as the Lancastrians' vaward advanced up the hill, towards the Great Eleanor Cross in the centre of the town, under a hail of Yorkist arrows:

> However, they [the Lancastrians] were compelled to turn back by a few archers who met them near the Great Cross, and to flee in disgrace to the west end of the town, where, entering by a lane which leads from that end northwards as far as St Peters Street, they had there a great fight with a certain small band of people of the king's army. Then, after not a few had been killed on both sides, going out onto the heath called Barnet Heath, lying near the north end of the town, they had a great battle with certain large forces, perhaps four or five thousand, of the vanguards of the king's army. The southern men, who were fiercer at the

beginning were broken quickly afterwards, and the more quickly because looking back, they saw no one coming up from the main body of the king's army, or preparing to bring them help, whereupon they turned their backs on the northern men and fled. And the northern men seeing this pursued them very swiftly on horseback; and catching a good many of them, ran them through with their lances.[17]

When the Lancastrians reached the Yorkist vaward position on Barnet Heath, the 5,000 strong battle, and especially the specialist Burgundian gunners, were still in the process of turning to face their flank. Gregory, possibly in the main battle at Sandridge with Warwick, saw the defensive contraptions they had to move and realign into position and the confusion that resulted from the manoeuvre:

And before the gunners and Burgundians could level their guns they were busily fighting, and many a gun of war was provided that was of little avail or none at all, for the Burgundians had such instruments that would shoot both pellets of lead and arrows of an ell in length with six feathers, three in the middle, and three at one end, with a very large head of iron at the other end, and wild fire, all together. In time of need they could not shoot one of them, for the fire turned back on those who would shoot these three things. Also they had nets made of great cords of four fathoms long and four feet wide, like a hedge, at every second knot there was a nail standing upright, so that no man could pass over it without the likelihood of being hurt. Also they had a pavise [a large wooden shield] borne as a door, made with a staff folding up and down to set the pavise where they like, and loop holes with shooting windows to shoot out at. And when their shot was spent and finished, they cast the pavise before them, then no man might come over the pavise because of the nails that stood upright, unless he wished to do himself a mischief. Also they had a thing made like a lattice full of nails as the net was, but it could be moved as a man would, a man might squeeze it together so that the length would be more than two yards long, and if he wished, he might pull it wide, so that it would be four square. And that served to lie at gaps where horsemen could enter in, and many a caltrop. And as the real opinion of worthy men who will not dissemble or curry favour for any bias, they could not understand that all these devices did any good or harm, except on our side with King Henry. Therefore they are much neglected, and men betake themselves to mallets of lead, bows, swords, glaives and axes.[18]

Gregory's graphic contempt for the innovative defences and temperamental handguns of Warwick's mercenaries is plain enough yet, if they had not been hastily realigned, the Lancastrians might have lost the battle or alternatively found it very difficult to come to grips with their enemy. However, Gregory does not explain the reason for the Yorkist mainward at Sandridge not supporting the hard-pressed vaward at the crucial moment, which, according to Whethamstede, stood idle, watching the battle's outcome.

The Yorkists were not the only ones with problems at the second battle of St Albans, as Gregory's observations highlight that, on the Lancastrian side,

The substance that got the field were household men and feed men. I ween there were not 5,000 men that fought in the queen's party, for the most part of the northern men fled away, and some were taken and spoiled out of their harness by the way as they fled. And some of them robbed ever as they went, a pitiful thing it is to hear it.[19]

So how did the Lancastrians, with such desertion problems of their own, break the Yorkist four-mile-long battle-line? From Gregory and Whethamstede's eyewitness accounts it is possible, given the unique details of the battle, to isolate the reasons why the second battle of St Albans was such a disaster for the Earl of Warwick, and how the Lancastrians were able to turn a carefully prepared defensive array into a panic-stricken running mêlée.

Three separate attacks are mentioned, each Yorkist detachment receiving little or no information from 'scourers' or messengers about where the enemy was at a given time, until it was too late. The first attack by the Lancastrians at the Great Cross probably caught the Yorkists by surprise, but then the indomitable Trollope sent a larger force to attempt to dislodge the Yorkist archers there by outflanking them farther up the street. Here the Lancastrians met with another Yorkist contingent, which was scattered after a 'great fight', which in turn made the archers' position at the Great Cross untenable. After clearing the town, the Lancastrians approached the turning Yorkists on Barnet Heath, who at first put up stiff resistance. However, the battle-hardened veterans of the north broke them quickly due to the Yorkist mercenaries' malfunctioning weapons and, more important, because of their forced realignment and lack of support from Warwick's battle. One can only assume that the Kingmaker commanding the mainward was some distance from the vaward when it was attacked, and that, by the time he reached Sandridge from his original position at Nomansland Common, the unfortunate men of the vaward were already looking over their shoulders and were on the verge of collapse. Thinking it wise to save what troops he still had left, Warwick may have decided to quit the field there and then. With darkness falling he did just that, leaving the routed vaward at the mercy of the jubilant Lancastrian 'spears'.

The queen's highly disciplined force of 'household men and feed men' – containing the retainers of such nobles as Somerset, Exeter, Northumberland, Devon and Shrewsbury, and many of the fiercer northern lords such as Clifford, Roos, Greystoke and Welles. This force in the end proved too much for the less experienced Yorkists in what turned out to be a commander's nightmare for the Earl of Warwick – bad intelligence in the face of the enemy on too wide a front.

After the second battle of St Albans, Warwick attempted to blame his defeat on the treachery of a man called Lovelace, caught at Wakefield and given his life by the Lancastrians on the pretext of playing the traitor to the Yorkist cause. This smacks of a cover up to his blunder. In fact the whole Lovelace story comes from the pen of Jean de Waurin, who, meeting with Warwick some time after Towton, may have been fed by the Kingmaker with some material for his history. Also, if Warwick needed further security for this kind of fabrication, most of the men who were with him at St Albans, such as Norfolk and Fauconberg, were conveniently dead by this time, not to mention the lords instantly beheaded by the Lancastrians after the battle in the usual reprisals that now became commonplace in the Wars of the Roses.

When Warwick's forces capitulated, the queen saw to it that the young Prince of Wales judged and saw to the executions of Lord Bonville, a mortal enemy of the Earl of Devon, and Sir Thomas Kyriell, a veteran of the French Wars, in an effort to dissuade her son from assimilating the weak and feeble nature of her husband. He was just seven years old at the time. When the king was eventually found, laughing and singing under a tree, Andrew Trollope, limping from a wound received from a Yorkist caltrop, was knighted by the young prince for his services. Trollope is reputed to have nonchalantly exclaimed, 'My lord, I have not deserved it for I slew no more than fifteen men. I stood still in one place and they came unto me, but they stayed with me.'[20] A fitting, if not cavalier-like, end to a battle that was won, in part, due to Trollope's tactical advice in combination, perhaps, with the Duke of Somerset's authority, plus a little luck, of course.

With Warwick on the run and the road to London open at last, the sweet smell of success lifted Lancastrian spirits, even though reports were coming in daily that Edward, Duke of York, was marching on the capital at the head of an army fresh from his victory in the west.

Queen Margaret wisely withdrew her main army to Dunstable, as by now the reputation of the 'northmen' was preceding all before it, and she sent a contingent of hand-picked men to London's Aldgate, where they demanded admission in the king's name. The mayor refused, as the citizens 'living in mykel dread'[21] of the pillaging stories of Warwick's earlier propaganda campaign were in no mood to fall for such a trick, even though it was their king who craved admittance. Earlier the commons had destroyed some carts carrying food and supplies to the Lancastrian army and had also risen against certain knights who were at Westminster on the queen's behalf. The fickle citizens reacted on the mayor's orders that everyone was to stay indoors under curfew, and, at length, the hard-pressed mayor was ordered by the queen to proclaim the Duke of York a traitor. However, the city held out under these pressures and, in the end, negotiations broke down when news of the approaching Yorkist army reached London.

With the queen's army on the verge of total desertion through lack of victuals, the ambitions of the Lancastrian house sadly crumbled. If London had been taken by force of arms, circumstances might have been different, but the queen chose not to press the issue, possibly because of the dispersal of the Lancastrian contingents, and perhaps because to disband and reform her forces afresh was a much better option than to conduct a battle and ultimately a siege with a ragged and unruly army. By the end of February 1461 the king, the queen and the remnants of their scattered northern army were on their way back to Yorkshire.

As they went homewards they continued plundering the country –

taking men's carts, horses and cattle – so that, by all accounts, men of the shires that they passed had almost no beasts left to till their land. It is also reported that some towns that had been ravaged by Queen Margaret's troops found it very difficult to recover from this midwinter foraging, although it is difficult to assess whether the scale of the 'disaster' was a product of Yorkist propaganda.

The war between north and south was to continue, but with a new slant in the form of a man who was prepared, with the help of his followers, to usurp the English throne. Unlike his father, Richard, Duke of York, Edward was no longer prepared to keep faith with his enemies – his father's killers – or the king. However, he saw the means, with Warwick's political prowess, if not his military ability, to assert his own character on the Londoners in the guise of a medieval saviour, now that they were desperate for deliverance. He was about not only to bring his father's claims back to life, but also to surpass them, fighting the bloodiest battle on British soil in the process.

THREE

The Rose of Rouen

After the second battle of St Albans the Earl of Warwick, and the remnants of his routed army, immediately marched to link up with Edward, Duke of York, who had already heard of the Lancastrian threat facing London because of the earl's defeat. William Worcester recorded where the two men eventually met, what the composition of Edward's force was (the named lords all fighting for him at Towton) and how, with the political help of the Nevilles, Edward Plantagenet was acclaimed King of England:

> When he heard this news, Edward, the new Duke of York, who was then near Gloucester, hastened towards London, and at Chipping Norton, in Oxfordshire, met the Earl of Warwick. And then there were in the army of the Duke Edward, Walter Devereux, William Herbert, John Wenlock, William Hastings and many others of the Welsh Marches, with 8,000 armed men. And they entered London with him and Edward stayed at his home at Baynard's Castle.
>
> On the Sunday following [1 March], after midday, in the big field at Clerkenwell the populace of the city congregated together with the army of the Duke to the number of 3,000 or 4,000, whom the said reverend father George Neville, then Chancellor of England, ordered to stand in the field. And he caused to be proclaimed the title by which the said Edward could claim the crown of England and France, and at once all the people shouted that Edward was and should be king. I was there and heard this, and I went down with them at once into the city.[1]

It takes little imagination to visualize what happened in St John's Field when:

> Unto the host were proclaimed certain articles and points that King Henry had offended in, whereupon it was demanded of the said people

[in the presence of the army] whether the said Henry were worthy to reign as king any longer or no. Whereupon the people cried hugely and said 'Nay, Nay'. And after it was asked of them whether they would have the Earl of March for their king and they cried with one voice 'Yea, Yea'.[2]

Stage managed by the chancellor and his brother Warwick this might have been, but in the eyes of the people of London it was a blessing after everything they had endured over the past few weeks. However, Edward's position was still far from secure, chiefly because most of the nobles were with the king in the north. Also, even though London was prepared to acknowledge a new monarch, the threat of these Lancastrian forces looming on the horizon could seriously undermine Edward's fragile authority if he did not strike at once to eradicate it. To this end Edward wasted no time in accepting the crown at Baynard's Castle. Worcester described the speed at which all this took place:

On the third day of March the Archbishop of Canterbury, the Bishops of Salisbury and Exeter, and John Duke of Norfolk, Richard Earl of Warwick, Lord Fitzwalter, William Herbert, Lord Ferrers of Chartley [then Sir Walter Devereux] and many others held a council at Baynard's Castle, where they agreed and decided that Edward, Duke of York should be King of England. And on the fourth day of March the Lord Edward, Duke of York went publicly to Westminster with the lords and was received with a procession. After the declaration of his title, he took the crown and sceptre of St Edward, and caused himself to be proclaimed Edward IV.[3]

The new king began his reign on Wednesday 4 March 1461. However, the enthronement ceremony was deferred until a later date, as, according to George Neville, more important things had to be put in order first. In fact in true medieval fashion some chronicles tell us that Edward wished to be judged worthy of the crown, by God himself, in battle before his coronation. It is more likely that quite simply the Yorkists did not want to waste any time, and instead decided to strike at the Lancastrians as soon as possible rather than keep nobles in London who might be better employed gathering recruits in their own 'countries' for the inevitable march north. To this end, on the Saturday after the Te Deum was sung at Westminster Abbey, King Edward despatched Warwick northward 'with a great band of men', after already sending the Duke of Norfolk 'into his country [East Anglia] with all diligence to prepare for the war on the party of King Edward'.[4] Norfolk was sent to recruit troops on the first day after Edward was proclaimed king, a clear indication of the urgency placed on the forthcoming campaign, and an urgency that was to become a keynote of the events leading up to the battle of Towton. This was a further example of Edward's aptitude for initiating speedy action, if not also showing his unabated thirst for revenge on his family's killers.

According to George Neville, Warwick, Norfolk, Edward and Lord Fauconberg 'took different roads'[5] to their agreed meeting place in the north, which suggests that the next departure after Warwick and Norfolk from London on 11 March was commanded by Fauconberg. Hearne's Fragment, which describes some events in the Towton campaign, gives details of the Yorkist order of march:

> Where as on the Wednesday next following the king's footmen assembled in a great number, of the which the most part were Welshmen and Kentishmen. Then on the Friday ensuing, King Edward issued out of the city in goodly order, at Bishopgate, it then being the 12th day of March [13th according to George Neville] and held on his journey, following this other.[6]

The footmen assembled on the Wednesday and, captained by the veteran Lord Fauconberg, were to become the vaward, the front advance guard of the army. The vaward, usually containing the most men, was in this case a day's march ahead of the main body of men commanded by the king, due to the long snaking supply wagons that must have accompanied the troops to war in those days. Estimates on the length of baggage trains, and how vulnerable and unwieldy they were, are given in the extreme by a Hungarian historian, G. Perjes. Using his calculations, based on large armies of the seventeenth century with provisions to last a month, an army of 60,000 would require a wagon train of 11,000 carts, 22,000 drivers and helpers and 50,000 to 70,000 draught animals, all in a single-file exodus calculated as stretching 198 kilometres, with the rear being behind the head of the column by eight days. Dividing this by six to approximate the

10,000-odd troops in Fauconberg's vaward, we may surmise the resulting 33 km baggage train to be a great burden on the march.

In reality, though, as John Gillingham points out in his excellent military study of the Wars of the Roses, armies probably only had a few days' supply to carry in far fewer wagons, the majority of their food being provided by paid victuallers travelling with the army, town 're-fuelling stops' and through the dangerous practice of living off the land. This latter method of obtaining supplies was a great problem to army commanders as it could lead to the risky dispersal of one's foragers, as at the battle of Wakefield in 1460, and in extreme cases to the unruly actions of pillage, which Queen Margaret's army resorted to during their march on London.

In accepting these difficulties it is therefore obvious that towns and villages were essential staging posts to marching Wars of the Roses armies, because not only did they provide better billeting facilities for some of the soldiers, but also, and more important, they supplied them with what they needed to continue. This, as one can imagine, was equally problematical for a town's citizens when an influx of such vast numbers of men and animals presented themselves at their gates. It is to this end that King Edward secured immense loans, not only to pay his men with but also to buy food and supplies on the march north as well. Indeed his troops were ordered to refrain from robbery, sacrilege and rape 'on pain of death', in great contrast, if not clever Yorkist propaganda, to counter the Lancastrian scorched earth retreat a few weeks earlier.

Edward's own line of march took him through St Albans and Cambridge, with what appears to have been a north-westerly change of direction in response to news, according to Jean de Waurin's Chronicle, that Henry VI was based at Nottingham. One would have thought that the direct road to the north through Newark would have been a more natural route for the Yorkists, but, according to the Burgundian chronicler, Edward's army reached Nottingham on 22 March and here received further reports that the Lancastrians had retreated into Yorkshire beyond the River Aire. Judging by the earlier news that the enemy was near, it may be safe to assume that Edward IV linked up with the forces of the Earl of Warwick before he reached Yorkshire in anticipation of a Lancastrian army in the vicinity. However, the Duke of Norfolk's forces may still have been some distance behind them both at this time.

The Armies

The 'Rose of Rouen', a Yorkist political poem of the era, alludes to which nobles, towns and shires made up Edward's army once united later at the battle of Towton. The nobles' names are identified by their livery badges, 'The Rose' being Edward IV. (Edward was born on 28 April 1442 at Rouen in France while his father was on campaign there.):

For to save all England The Rose did his intent,
With Calais and with London with Essex and with Kent,
And all the south of England up to the water of Trent,
And when he saw the time best The Rose from London went.
Blessed be the time, that ever God spread that flower!

The way into the north country The Rose full fast he sought,
With him went The Ragged Staff [Earl of Warwick] that many men there
   brought,
So did The White Lion [Duke of Norfolk] full worthily he wrought,
Almighty Jesus bless his soul, that their armies taught.
Blessed be the time, that ever God spread that flower!

The Fish Hook [Lord Fauconberg] came to the field in full eager mood,
So did The Cornish Chough [Lord Scrope of Bolton] and brought forth
   all her brood,
There was The Black Ragged Staff [Lord Grey of Ruthin] that is both
   true and good,
The Bridled Horse [Sir William Herbert], The Water Bouget [Viscount
   Bouchier] by The Horse stood [Earl of Arundel].
Blessed be the time, that ever God spread that flower!

The Greyhound [Sir Walter Devereux], The Harts Head [Lord Stanley]
   they quit them well that day,
So did The Harrow of Canterbury and Clinton [Lord Clinton] with his
   Key,
The White Ship of Bristol he feared not the fray,
The Black Ram of Coventry he said not one nay,
Blessed be the time, that ever God spread that flower!

The Falcon and the Fetterlock [Edward IV as Duke of York] was there
    that tide,
The Black Bull [Sir William Hastings] also himself would not hide,
The Dolphin [Lord Audley] came from Wales, Three Corbies [Sir Roger
    Corbie] by his side,
The proud Leopard of Salisbury gaped his eyes wide.
Blessed be the time, that ever God spread that flower!

The Wolf came from Worcester, full sore he thought to bite,
The Dragon came from Gloucester, he bent his tail to smite,
The Griffen came from Leicester, flying in as tight,
The George came from Nottingham, with spear for to fight,
Blessed be the time, that ever God spread that flower![7]

In addition to the nobles mentioned above we must include such men as
Sir John Wenlock, Sir John Dinham, Sir Walter Blount, John de la Pole, Sir
Humphrey Stafford, Lord Grey of Wilton, Lord Saye and Sele, Lord
Abergavenny, Lord Dudley, Lord Cobham, Sir Robert Ogle, Lord
Fitzwalter, Lord Stourton, Sir Richard Croft, Sir Roger Tocotes, Sir Thomas
Vaughan, Sir John Dunne, Sir John Say, Sir William Stanley, Sir James
Strangeways, Sir John Scott, Robert Horne Esquire, John Stafford, Sir
Thomas Montgomery, Sir John Howard, Sir Thomas Walgrave, Sir John
Fogge, Sir Laurence Rainsford, Sir Robert Harcourt, Sir John Paston and
the rest of the Bouchier clan, notably William and Humphrey.

A great proportion of these men received their advancements after the
battle of Towton. However, before this we may wonder what motivated
such men at arms, in both Yorkist and Lancastrian armies, to join one side
or the other. Politics are obviously the main reasons behind the nobles'
choice of camps, but, because of this, the peers' retainers and consequently
the troops that the man at arms recruited rarely had this choice in general
terms during the fifteenth century. Therefore they landed on one side or
the other purely out of loyalty.

The nobles and knights with their retinues formed the backbone of a
typical Wars of the Roses army in an age when loyalty in the field was a
matter of payment and/or allegiance. It was loyalty in this form that made
or broke a battle line when, in some instances, as we have seen, treachery
and double-dealing could be bought or sold without warning. In reality,

though, it was never as clear cut as this because, when battle was joined, commanders or 'captains' could do very little to alter the inevitable, except lead their contingents by example or display personal feats of arms to encourage their troops. It was the men themselves who dictated whether they ran or stayed put, according to their status or their loyalty. However, this apparent loyalty did not deter some men from tempering this allegiance with what has become known as 'trimming', in other words working on both sides of the fence until a favourable turn of events presented itself, namely being on the winning side. The Stanleys were elitist in this particular area, as at the battle of Blore Heath and later at Bosworth Field, but, curiously enough, neither brother displayed this action in the Towton campaign under Edward IV.

Most knights, including the king, were trained in the use of arms from an early age by henchmen, and it was this training that in the end would be put to the test on the battlefield at the pinnacle of their careers. In fact it was this very act of violence in battle that was longed for by the knight, it being the culmination of his life, through which he might be noted and receive rewards and advancement on the social and political scale. This was the knight's reason for being in a battle on the right side and also, if he needed it, the justification for unlawfully killing his fellow Englishman when lawful killing was religiously condoned only when the victims were enemies of the king or the Church. However, to explain why the nobles took one side or the other in the Wars of the Roses, or neither in some cases, we must look at the methods of raising English armies in the fifteenth century, as part of the answer lies there.

To begin with, the strong king in the eyes of his followers was the epitome of the medieval knight of Arthurian legends or the great sagas, pious in his beliefs and strong in battle. He was also the greatest rallying point for his nobles' loyalty, greed and ambition. In 1341 Edward III reorganized the structure of the armies that left England to fight in France. He instituted a system of written indentured contracts between the Crown and the prominent nobles of the land. These nobles, like the Earls of Warwick or Northumberland, for example, would then subcontract with knights and men at arms who were their friends, tenants and neighbours. These were the great captains' retainers, in other words professional soldiers who were raised and paid by, and who fought with, such captains as a team under their banners, following their lord and king against his enemies whenever they were called on to do so. They were all, in essence – in addition to the king's household of fifty or so, and the border garrisons – the standing English army of the day. Some of these captains were, even in 1461, 'of the war of France', that is experienced professional fighters, and as such were valued leaders not only as veterans, but also as military tacticians. Men such as William Neville, Lord Fauconberg – at sixty years of age at the battle of Towton – were indispensable assets to the army and, as such, Edward IV must have relied heavily on their knowledge. It also shows how important these men were, when Englishman fought Englishman at home, in the fact that some veterans had already been systematically killed in the course of the Wars of the Roses to deprive one side of further help in such military matters.

The above system of recruitment was called 'Livery and Maintenance' and was the culmination of 'bastard feudalism', which also involved, by the time of the Wars of the Roses, a contract clause stating that, in return for the nobles' protection, that is to champion the retainers' personal quarrels from the law courts to the battlefield, the retainer in gratitude had to take the field under the noble's banner, wear his livery – for instance the White Ragged Staff badge of Warwick on a red jacket – and fight for him when called on to do so.

In the Hundred Years War the system worked well under strong kingship, but, when the English lands in France were at last overrun and the weak King Henry VI showed his inability to rule, things went badly wrong. England was at first infiltrated by disgruntled soldiers returning home from the war to find employment in the only trade they knew. They took the opportunities offered by Livery and Maintenance and sought employment, payment and protection with the great nobles, whose resulting private armies became powerful forces, extremely dangerous to the king and in turn weakening his authority. The king's only protection in such a volatile situation was to gain as much support from his nobles as possible through patronage and advancement, which consequently bred discontent similar to the York–Somerset feud in the early days of the Wars of the Roses. These sorts of divisions between the nobles counterbalanced the equilibrium of law and order, and created the polarities that became a cause and such a feature of the Wars of the Roses when one noble received greater rewards than the other.

Thus there was not a clear-cut reason why each noble or knight chose York or Lancaster, as it was the more complicated question of retaining that caused one side to be favoured more than the other. In such a predicament, ancient land quarrels, such as those enacted between the Nevilles and the Percys, even turned local issues into miniature wars and forced both families onto opposing sides during the Wars of the Roses.

Some nobles, however, chose not to obey the rules of Livery and Maintenance. The Paston Family, whose letters still survive, fought for the Duke of Norfolk as retainers. John Paston was summoned by the Duke in 1485 to do him service:

> and that ye bring with you such a company of tall men as ye may goodly make at my cost and charge . . . and I pray you ordain them jackets of my livery, and I shall content you at your meeting with me.[8]

In this event, however, it is very unlikely that Paston complied with the order because, soon after Bosworth and the death of the Duke of Norfolk on the field, Paston was appointed sheriff of the county. Here then we have an instance of a knight not obeying his lord in a risk that might have turned out quite differently if Richard III had defeated Henry Tudor in battle and later sought Paston out to punish him.

Apart from the complicated and unsavoury methods of Livery and Maintenance that were used to recruit support, another equally domineering way that a Wars of the Roses army used to supplement its numbers was to call out the militia and local shire levies under Commissions of Array. The 'Rose of Rouen' gives details of which towns and counties sent contingents of troops to fight for Edward IV at the battle of Towton. When the Earl of Warwick left London in early March, he was given the authority by the king, dated 8 March, to raise levies from Northamptonshire, Warwickshire, Leicestershire, Staffordshire, Worcestershire, Gloucestershire, Shropshire, Nottinghamshire, Derbyshire and Yorkshire, thereby corroborating some of the details in the poem.

These Commissions of Array gave the Earl of Warwick, and the other Yorkist captains, the power to recruit all men between the ages of sixteen and sixty years from the shires in defence of the realm. This method of raising troops was Anglo–Saxon in origin and involved every man's promised allegiance to his king. Failure to respond in some instances, and in times of great need, meant forfeiture and death. In fact the reason why such large armies were engaged at the battle of Towton is because two kings used their equal powers of Commissions of Array to supplement their nobles' retinues. If we take a Lancastrian array, for instance when the city of York sent 1,000 men to 'the lamentable battle of Towton',[9] we may be able to get a feel for just how large both armies were. Certainly the Yorkist army was huge by the standards of the day and it is recorded that Edward raised more men than any English king had put in the field before. The Lancastrian force was even greater.

Traditionally, however, Wars of the Roses armies were much smaller than at Towton, at most about 5,000 to 10,000 men, sometimes a lot less, who resulted from combination of the above methods of recruitment. Typical of shire and city levies of the era is the Bridport Muster Roll, which formed part of a Commissions of Array in 1457, mustering in all over 12,000 men from southern England for Henry VI. The individuals listed for Bridport in Dorset provide an all too rare glimpse of our medieval ancestors' state of military readiness against the king's enemies, in this case French raiding parties on the English coast.

Of armed men, by far the greatest proportion were equipped with the longbow, the most devastating weapon of the day. Most of these men carried a sheaf (twenty-four) or part sheaf of cloth yard (30 in) arrows and a buckler (a small round shield). Second only to the bow and arrow was a sword, buckler and dagger. Most men wore various styles of sallet and kettle helmets. Even an earlier type of helmet, a basinet, was owned by one man. Wealthier men were ordered to provide more weapons or armour if they could to supplement the rest of the militia who were deficient in arms. Other sorts of weapons were also inspected at Bridport, such as various polearms, including glaives, spears, bills and the lethal two-handed knightly killing tool the poleaxe. Even a primitive handgun was noted.

'Harness', meaning the complement of a man's military equipment, also included full defensive plate armour. It is clear from the muster roll, however, that bits and pieces of the full suit of armour or 'cap à pie' had been acquired by the soldiers along the way, while on their travels, as family heirlooms or, more recently, on the battlefields of France. In Bridport, for instance, leg harness gauntlets, chain harness and the more popular padded 'jack' and brigandine of the period were all in use. A few pavises, similar to the ones used at the second battle of St Albans, were also recorded in the muster, and more were ordered to be made.

The traditional medieval shield was absent, in preference to the buckler, which is significant given that most soldiers would have required two hands to do their job on the battlefield, such as pull a longbow or wield a cut-and-thrust weapon. The knight or man at arms on foot, usually encased in armour plate, eventually rejected his trusty 'heater' shield because of this, in favour of the two-handed pole weapon and greater manoeuvrability in combat. The notion that a mid-fifteenth-century man in armour was an immobile automaton waddling aimlessly around the battlefield is a well-worn untruth. A medieval manuscript of the period depicts a knight in full armour-plate doing a cartwheel to illustrate the point.

The Bridport Muster of 1457 also begs the question of how large Wars of the Roses armies were at the time. We can see that, on this occasion, the southern counties alone were able to raise 12,000 men between them in defence of the realm. What size of army was then available to the Yorkists and Lancastrians in 1461, when the whole of England, and parts of Wales, Scotland and the continent were involved?

In summarizing the different ways of raising troops in the fifteenth century the hardest area to pinpoint, and thus completely understand the involvement of, is that of the mercenaries, who were employed in both Yorkist and Lancastrian ranks in the Wars of the Roses. These soldiers of fortune, whether Burgundian, French, Breton, Flemish or German, were specialists with their chosen weapons, but they would only fight while the money lasted. As we have seen so far, ad hoc units of mercenaries had failed badly in some engagements. At Mortimers Cross in 1461, for example, various nationalities of men were present in the Lancastrian army, which in the end may have suffered defeat because of them. However, Warwick's 'gunners and Burgundians' at the second battle of St Albans were unlucky, as flakes of snow may have caused their handguns to malfunction, some backfiring and killing their operators in the process. A contingent of Burgundians is also said to have been present at Towton, commanded by Seigneur de la Barde, but, judging by the weather on Palm Sunday 1461, we must also assume that the professionals had the same difficulties with their handguns then.

Later in the Wars of the Roses, Edward IV found his alliance with Burgundy useful at a crucial stage in his reign, in that the force with which he invaded England in 1471 contained as many as three hundred Flemish handgunners, nearly a quarter of his entire force. Even later, French mercenaries were present in Henry Tudor's army at the battle of Bosworth, but the most heroic 'stand' of mercenaries occurred in 1487 at the battle of

Stoke, when German and Swiss contingents in the Earl of Lincoln's army, commanded by Martyn Swartz, were destroyed to a man by Henry VII's forces in a vain attempt to put a Yorkist pretender on the throne.

With the addition of the standing Calais garrison, and the other border garrisons, these, then, were the available troops in the Wars of the Roses. As discussed, the reasons behind why they became part of one contingent or another varied, according to their status, loyalties, the effect of medieval press-ganging and just downright greed or hatred for the opposition. The effect of certain methods of recruitment on the common soldier is therefore very important when assessing a medieval warrior's 'battle attitude', that is how a man, taken from the land or a town, or recruited as a retainer or professional, might react to a given situation in the field. Much like all human experience of warfare, in some respects, it is not just the commander who influences his soldiers' feelings and reactions at a point of danger. A more direct effect on a soldier is his questioning why he is in such a situation in the first place, coupled with his strength of discipline. These factors more than any other make him stand or flee to the rear when the tide of battle turns, but more of this later.

The March North

When Edward united with the forces of Warwick and Fauconberg on the road to York, he learned that the Kingmaker had already disposed of his own father's killer while recruiting in Coventry. Warwick arrested the Bastard of Exeter there and promptly had him executed for the death of the Earl of Salisbury after the battle of Wakefield, which may have greatly encouraged the burgesses of the town to supply him with eighty militiamen, promising that forty more would follow. John Benet's Chronicle tells us that the Earl of Warwick marched to Lichfield with his recruits, then on to Doncaster to effect a meeting with King Edward, who Benet says had advanced through Newark. This is further evidence of the more direct line of march theory mentioned earlier, which in retrospect is a more reasonable assumption if we have to make a judgement on Edward's route north.

At a Yorkist council of war, still deficient of one prominent captain, John Mowbray, Duke of Norfolk, it was decided to advance without further delay into enemy territory, where Edward may, in theory at least, still have been able to recruit more support, although this is doubtful considering the massive Lancastrian presence in the Yorkshire area. As long as the Yorkist scouts were thorough in their intelligence, Edward's plan was to march on to Pontefract Castle, as the next formidable river behind which the Lancastrian strength might gather was the Aire. Using Pontefract's great fortification as a base, Edward may have chosen to wait for the Duke of Norfolk's contingents there, because the greatest concern in Yorkist minds at this time must have been the duke's lateness. Possibly even his loyalty was questioned as well. Coupled with these doubts was the fact that John Mowbray was terminally ill. What price his support before a major encounter with the Lancastrians? Nevertheless, the Yorkists reached Pontefract on or about 27 March 1461, and, according to tradition, made camp on a triangular piece of land below the castle on the Knottingley road known as Bubwith Heath. This tract of land is still visible and was situated behind what was Bubwith House. Relics of the period are said to have been found in the area during the last century.

Unfortunately we have no contemporary accounts of Lancastrian movements at this time. No documents survive similar to the 'Rose of Rouen', nor indeed do Henry VI's Commissions of Array, except for the city of York, Beverley and some isolated knights, which detail Lancastrian recruiting drives in 1461. We do know, however, that the Lancastrian headquarters was in York or its immediate area, as might have been expected, and that men must have been flocking to the king's standard for at least a month after the second battle of St Albans on 17 February. The Lancastrians, however, would not have kept such a large army standing for all that time, and promised allegiance would have been the order of the day up to the time when news came in that the enemy was near.

Thankfully, as an alternative means of assessing King Henry's 'captains' at the battle of Towton, we have Edward IV's Act of Attainder on the then defeated Lancastrian host, dated in the first year of the king's reign, 1461 (see Appendix 1). The attainder gives the names of those who lost their lives on Palm Sunday and includes the Duke of Somerset and others who were still on the run after the battle. The main protagonists for the king were the Dukes of Somerset and Exeter, the Earls of Devon and Northumberland, Viscount William Beaumont, Lord Roos, Lord Clifford, Lord Welles, Lord Neville, Lord Willoughby, Sir Thomas Grey, Lord Rugemond-Grey, Lord Dacre, Sir Humphrey Dacre, Sir Philip Wentworth, Sir John Fortescue, Sir William Tailboys, Sir Edmund Moundford, Sir Thomas Tresham, Sir William Vaux,

Sir Edward Hampden, Sir Thomas Fyndern, Sir John Courtenay, Sir Henry Lewes, Sir Nicholas Latimer, Sir John Heron, Sir Richard Tunstall, Sir Henry Bellingham, Sir Robert Whitingham, Sir John Butler, Sir William Mille, Sir Simon Hammes, Sir William Holland, Sir Thomas Butler and Sir Thomas Everingham. We may also assume from other evidence that the Earl of Wiltshire, Lord Scales (later made Earl Rivers by Edward IV), Lord Hungerford, Lord Mauley, Sir Ralph Grey, Sir Robert Hildyard, Sir William Plumpton, Sir Nicholas Harvey, Sir William Gascoigne, Sir Andrew Trollope and his brother David Trollope were also present on the field. In some cases, such as that of Sir William Gascoigne, there is no evidence of his fighting on the day. However, in Gascoigne's case, this point is very debatable, given that most of the Lancastrian strength was gathered, and that he had only just been knighted by the Earl of Northumberland after the battle of Wakefield. He was also present at the second battle of St Albans.

A surviving letter from King Henry VI to Sir William Plumpton, dated 13 March 1461, attests to this Yorkshire knight's presence at the battle of Towton at the cost of the life of his eldest son, who was killed there (see Appendix 2). The presence of other nobles, like the Earl of Wiltshire, can be confirmed as a result of their later captures, executions and subsequent attainders. It is at least safe to assume that anyone who had Lancastrian sympathies and personal scores to settle with the Yorkists was at this singular battle on Palm Sunday 1461.

The Lancastrian force mainly comprised northerners, but, judging by the nobles and the lesser-known squires listed in the Yorkist bill of attainder, men from all over the country were present in King Henry's army, including soldiers brought by the Earl of Devon from his own county and from Dorset, men from Nottingham, some from London, and others from Calais, France and Scotland. This proves that it was not a simple case of north or south, east or west, or 'red or white' that divided the houses of York and Lancaster, and it never was in the Wars of the Roses. In fact it may have been apparent, if Edward's Yorkists did arrive at Nottingham during their march north, that the Lancastrian king had deprived them of some, if not all, of the town's expected recruits. This makes the point that authority through Commissions of Array was by this time very much a case of who got there first to enlist support troops into compulsive or pressurized recruitment in whatever catchment area was available to them.

The Lancastrians soon quit York, their 'northern capital', and marched south-west, leaving the king – more at home with a bible than a poleaxe – the queen and the Prince of Wales in the city. This leading from the rear may have caused more than a little concern in the Lancastrian ranks, one might think, but none the less seems not to have damaged the nobles' confidence, although a great morale builder in medieval warfare must have been to have the King of England leading his men into battle, as the then king's father, Henry V, had done at Agincourt. Each soldier must instead have looked more to his immediate superior for orders, example and support in battle, rather than to the present king who was purely a figurehead by this time.

We can visualize that, as the Lancastrian dukes and lords strutted out of York beneath Micklegate Bar to fight for their king's reinstatement, their morale must have been high, if not overconfident, both in their numbers and their purpose to crush the new upstart Yorkist pretender, even without the king's presence in the field. The Duke of York's decomposing head spiked above them on the battlements, still there after the battle of Wakefield, must have added to their confidence in that it was they, the nobles, and not the king who had placed it there. Accounts of Lancastrian bravado state that the queen had ordered that room be left in this grisly company of Lancastrian trophies on Micklegate so that Edward and Warwick's heads might join them in time to come. Stories such as these were presumably intended to promote drive in the army, making it apparent that the Lancastrians were fighting on the 'right' side and that the Yorkist king was a rebel usurper of Henry's crown.

However, it is very difficult to get an impression of the common archer or billman's feelings as the two armies marched towards each other, although, as discussed, it must have been apparent in both camps that each side was fighting for a cause. Of greater concern to the soldiers must have been more basic feelings. William Gregory, the soldier who had witnessed medieval army life, gave an account of his own open contempt for the horsemen in the army, and the race for supplies of food before the second battle of St Albans:

> As for spearmen, they are only good to ride before the footmen and eat and drink up their victuals, and many more such pretty things they do. You must hold me excused for these expressions, but I say the best, for in the footmen is all the trust.[10]

Some of these 'footmen' may have been worried about payment for their services when much depended on their overcoming 'red tape' to receive the money they were owed. Issues such as how long they were to serve, how far they were to march, what would happen to their dependents while they were away and, ultimately, whether they would live or die, must have been fears visualized by veterans and raw recruits alike. Because of these feelings the commanders' eyes were firmly fixed on seeking a battle before these recruits, with their fickle ways, deserted when their forty days' service, or thereabouts, expired or when food and supplies had run out. This accounts for the eagerness of both armies to come to grips as quickly as possible, as delay could spell disaster on either side.

With this in mind the Lancastrians advanced on Tadcaster from York and eventually crossed the bridge over the River Wharfe, which, according to George Neville, was broken down in the process. Eventually the army took the old London road to the River Cock. Wading over this natural obstacle, which some authorities say was in full flood at the time, they gained the high ground immediately above and around the village of Towton and, placing watch on the edge of the high plateau overlooking Saxton village and the road from Ferrybridge, they sent out their 'scourers' to report Yorkist movements.

This was the Lancastrians' chosen ground. It is difficult to argue otherwise, as the tract of land that was to become the battlefield of Towton offered distinct advantages, as it is the highest land between Pontefract and York.

FOUR

'Let him fly that will, I will tarry with him that will tarry with me'

Ith these words the Earl of Warwick supposedly killed his horse with his sword, thereby claiming that from then on he would share the fate of the common soldier on foot, rather than having the means of taking to his horse in flight from the enemy when faced with defeat. Warwick's theatrical gesture comes from the pen of Edward Hall, crediting the Kingmaker with averting a major catastrophe in the Yorkist ranks immediately before or, depending on which way you look at it, after the battle of Ferrybridge. (Some historians regard the skirmish with Fitzwalter's men as 'the battle of Ferrybridge'.) Warwick's action (killing his horse) took place after this skirmish, but before what I consider to be the main battle.

The battle of Ferrybridge was somewhat of a dilemma for chroniclers in so much as most of the writers who considered the matter, and sadly there were few of them, failed to appreciate the sequence of events that were taking place so far north. In fact some authors could not differentiate between the battles of Ferrybridge and Towton, unaware even that they occurred on different days. The outcome of this confusion is that the bigger, and thus more important, battle of Towton has put Ferrybridge in its shadow. I hope to remedy this confusing situation here and hopefully to show that this singular engagement across a natural defensible obstacle ranks among the more acclaimed and interesting battles of the Wars of the Roses.

In discussing the authorities first, we learn that no sooner had the Yorkists reached Pontefract than Edward despatched a small force under the command of John Radcliffe, Lord Fitzwalter, to seize and hold the ferrybridge over the River Aire. Thus one of the crossings (the other being at Castleford) was secured for a Yorkist advance when news of the Duke of Norfolk's contingents was received. George Neville, in his letter to Coppini, the pro-Yorkist Papal Legate, wrote:

And at length on Palm Sunday, near a town called Ferrybridge, about sixteen miles from York, our enemies were routed and broken in pieces. Our adversaries had broken the bridge which was our way across, and were strongly posted on the other side, so that our men could only cross by a narrow way which they had made themselves after the bridge was broken. But our men forced a way by the sword, and many were slain on both sides. Finally the enemy took to flight, and very many of them were slain as they fled.[1]

William Gregory recorded that the battle of Ferrybridge took place on 28 March, 'Palm Sunday eve', and that 'Lord Fitzwalter was slain at Ferrybridge, and many with him were slain and drowned. And the Earl of Warwick was hurt in his leg with an arrow.'[2] In Hearne's Fragment, however, the chronicler states that it was Edward's 'foreprickers' (scouts) who were attacked at Ferrybridge, resulting in 'a great skirmish' in which Fitzwalter was killed.[3]

It seems probable that, apart from George Neville's confusing dates and Gregory's 'Palm Sunday eve' (placing an almost end-of-the-day stamp on events), the crossing at Ferrybridge was disputed between the early morning and the afternoon of 28 March. Obviously time was needed for Edward's army to reach Saxton enabling the Yorkists to fight on the 29th. It also seems likely that the Lancastrians broke the bridge down at Ferrybridge before the arrival of the Yorkist army at Pontefract on 27 March. According to Gregory the Yorkists, discovering this delaying tactic, may have then sent their 'foreprickers' out to rebuild a temporary crossing, as the road from Pontefract to Sherburn-in-Elmet and Tadcaster was the more direct line of march for Edward's army to York. Fitzwalter commanded this force, which promptly set to work either to build a pontoon across the river or, more likely, to straddle the destroyed bridge with planks of wood. This was 'the narrow way' that, according to George Neville, the Yorkists made themselves 'after the bridge was broken'.

Edward Hall, writing some seventy years later, gives a unique though uncorroborated account of what happened to Fitzwalter's men once they had rebuilt this makeshift bridge over the Aire. He also makes a tantalizing comparison between two of the young Lancastrian nobles, which later may have been the reason behind a baffling event:

Let no man think or yet imagine, that either the council of King Henry, or his vigilant queen, either neglected nor forgot to know or search what their enemies did, but that they prepared to their power all the men they either could persuade or allure to their purpose to take their part. And thus thinking themselves furnished, committed the governance of the army to the Duke of Somerset, the Earl of Northumberland and the Lord Clifford, as men desiring to revenge the death of their fathers slain at the first battle of St Albans. These noble captains, leaving King Henry, his wife and son for their safeguard in the city of York, passed the River Wharfe, with all their power, intending to prohibit King Edward to pass over the river Aire, and for the more expedition and exploit of their purpose, (after many comparisons were made between the Earl of Northumberland and the Lord Clifford, both being lusty in youth, and of frank courage) the Lord Clifford determined with his light horsemen, to make an assault to such as kept the passage of Ferrybridge, and so departed from the great army on the Saturday before Palm Sunday, and early before his enemies were awake, got the bridge, and slew the keepers of the same, and all such as would withstand him. The Lord Fitzwalter hearing the noise, suddenly rose out of his bed, and unarmed, with a poleaxe in his hand, thinking that it had been an affray amongst his men, came down to appease the same, but before he could say a word, or knew what the matter was, he was slain, and with him the Bastard of Salisbury, brother to the Earl of Warwick, a valiant young gentleman, and of great audacity.[4]

Lords Clifford, Northumberland and Somerset had much to prove in the Towton campaign. As previously discussed, all of their fathers had been systematically executed during the Duke of York's assault on St Albans in 1455. Clifford, however, was probably the most malicious of them all. He is reputed to have vowed, as some other nobles had, to kill all of the Duke of York's family for his father's sake, and to this end he commanded an elite body of men (his personal retainers), who also had scores to settle with the House of York. These were 'The Flower of Craven' – men from a district in which border war was part of everyday life – thus a hard and cruel reality had moulded them under John Clifford of Skipton's command. There is no doubt as to Clifford's courage and almost terminator-like attitude towards his mortal enemies, the Yorkists, but we must temper this bloody profile of him – after all, he was labelled 'The Butcher' – with the fact that these were very violent times when justice, chivalry and lawful killing in war became one and the same in a knight's professional career, especially when it affected his family ties.

On 28 March, Lord Clifford's force of cavalry, possibly five hundred spears, surprised and captured Ferrybridge and killed its keepers in an early morning raid on a Yorkist force that had obviously not taken adequate precautions against attack. The overall Lancastrian plan seems to have been to weaken the Yorkists by forcing them to attempt to dislodge them from a very difficult and defensible position across the river, and then to let them come up against their fresh, strong main army at Towton in a battle that would put the morale-battered Yorkists at a grave supply, as well as numerical, disadvantage. This sound tactical plan worked in part, but not before the expected encounter across the River Aire, in which many were killed on both sides.

When the bitterly cold day dawned, Warwick received news that the bridge had been captured and Fitzwalter's men killed. Exhausted and fearful of the consequences, he reported to Edward at Pontefract Castle. Edward Hall reported his story:

> When the Earl of Warwick was informed of this feat [Clifford's attack], he like a man desperate, mounted on his hackney, and came blowing to King Edward saying 'Sir I pray God have mercy on their souls, which in the beginning of your enterprise hath lost their lives, and because I see no success of the world, I remit the vengeance and punishment to God our creator and redeemer' and with that he alighted down and slew his horse with his sword, saying 'Let him fly that will, for surely I will tarry with him that will tarry with me' and he kissed the cross hilt of his sword.[5]

Warwick must have been thinking of the whole Yorkist army deserting there and then on hearing of this setback. The truth of the matter is that we must either regard the above incident as a typical, but clever, Warwick ploy, to reassure his troops publicly that he for one would not retreat as he had done at the second battle of St Albans, or we must disregard the story as being a figment of Edward Hall's vivid imagination. The fact is that the Yorkists immediately advanced towards the bridge to dispute it, and, according to George Neville, a 'great fight' ensued.

Jean de Waurin in his *Recueil des Chroniques d'Engleterre* fails to mention Fitzwalter's name at all in association with the Ferrybridge action, but he did provide an interesting unconfirmed military viewpoint of the battle manoeuvres there, although the nobles mentioned, plus the dates and times, are suspect. According to Waurin, after receiving news at Nottingham of the occupation of Ferrybridge by the Duke of Somerset and Earl Rivers (then Lord Scales) on the Friday before Palm Sunday, King Edward advanced to within 2 miles of the enemy and made camp, presumably at Pontefract,

> and as soon as they had made camp the Duke of Suffolk [in 1461 John de la Pole] sent a small company to find out the strength of the enemy, but they went so far forward that a guard saw them and raised the alarm. The small party was in so much danger of being routed that the Earl of March had to send reinforcements for his reconnaissance troops. They managed to push the enemy back to the bridge where they formed a defensive line. When the Earl of March heard about this he ordered all his council and troops to move closer to the enemy, and after he had made a new camp he went to see the situation with his commanders. After studying the enemies' positions the courageous and pious Earl of March declared it was necessary to gain the passage rapidly as they would not be able to press their advantage further otherwise. Therefore the order was given to attack the bridge which had been fortified by the enemy, and it so happened the battle lasted from midday to six o'clock in the evening and there died more than 3,000 men on both sides.[6]

The last historical evidence we need to examine before we make any assumptions about the battle over the River Aire is the crucial factor in Edward Hall's Chronicle regarding the reason for Lord Clifford's hasty withdrawal from Ferrybridge. This action, which effectively cleared the Lancastrians from their position, was attributed to the Yorkist vaward's threatened flank attack, thus, in Hall's account, who considered it a mere skirmish, dispelling with a major battle at all.

After Warwick had killed his horse in the presence of the army, Hall gave King Edward the role of Henry V at Agincourt. In a speech to his troops he gave his men a chance to depart, but promised that great rewards would be bestowed on those who stayed. He also added a codicil that soldiers would be paid double wages for killing deserters:

After this proclamation ended the Lord Fauconberg, Sir Walter Blount and Robert Horne with the foreward, passed the river at Castleford 3 miles from Ferrybridge, intending to have environed and enclosed Lord Clifford and his company, but they being thereof advertised, departed in great haste towards King Henry's army.[7]

Thus, according to the Tudor chronicler, the crossing was gained by a Fauconberg flank march that caused Clifford to panic and flee.

But where is the truth behind the heroic speeches and daring deeds on that bitterly cold March day over the icy waters of the River Aire? The answers lie in the chronicles and in common sense, for, if we take away the obvious inconsistencies of time, dates, names and the preoccupation of putting theories into neat little boxes, not allowing for the unforeseen or the effects of chance, and apply instead other historical evidence, we can see the battle of Ferrybridge as it was – a major engagement preceded by a night raid, which very nearly destroyed Yorkist plans completely.

First, if King Edward arrived in the vicinity of Pontefract on 27 March, knowing that the bridge across the River Aire was destroyed, it would have been imperative for him to send out a force to rebuild the crossing without delay. Avoiding a delay was, as always, central to a campaign's programme with regard to the ever-increasing problems of dwindling supplies within the army. Second, however, if the bridge was intact, this would have prompted the Yorkists to occupy it, in this instance to guard it for the army to cross over once they had been refreshed. However, this theory can be disproved if we take into account George Neville's letter to Coppini, which indicated that Ferrybridge was already broken down by the Lancastrians and that the Yorkists made a 'narrow way' to get across. It is very doubtful that the Yorkists made this makeshift bridge in the face of the enemy on 28 March. Therefore Neville's description of events points to a Yorkist force building a temporary crossing before Clifford and his retainers arrived on the scene. As discussed earlier, bridge-breaking was a common safety measure in the rear of a retreating army, as well as good tactics to harass an enemy's advance. It would be unreasonable to suggest that the Lancastrians did anything less than this during their march back to Yorkshire after the second battle of St Albans.

The bridge that had been destroyed by the Lancastrians 'beforehand' must have been quite substantial and was not, in 1461 at least, a ferry at all, although there is evidence that as early as 1070 there existed a temporary ferrybridge over the River Aire. The Brotherton paved landing was still visible when C. Forrest wrote his history of Knottingley in 1871. There is also mention that William the Conqueror crossed that way against the Northumbrians, later destroying the ferry.[8] In 1340, 1356, 1359 and 1362, grants of pontage (bridge repairs) were issued and bars had been built on a static bridge for tolls to be taken. This in itself proves that increased medieval traffic had by then made this an important crossing on the road to York. The Lancastrians therefore did well to sabotage the bridge in an effort to hold up the Yorkist march and thus put their next plan into operation.

In the early hours of Saturday 28 March, Lord Clifford's force made short work of Fitzwalter's 'engineers', apparently asleep at their posts, and in the brief skirmish most of the Yorkists were killed. Only Hall's Chronicle relates this story, but Hearne's Chronicle mentions 'foreprickers' and that of Waurin refers to a 'small company' who got too close to the enemy, which may substantiate Hall's claims. It seems that the Earl of Warwick was informed immediately of this disaster, probably by a survivor, and in turn reported to Edward who moved the Yorkist army forward in an effort to regain the bridge from Clifford. This was to become the main battle of Ferrybridge, not just the Fitzwalter skirmish as some historians have previously claimed. Clifford, according to Jean de Waurin, had fortified the narrow crossing and not only was the bridge a difficult objective to win, but also the land on the north bank of the Aire was easily defended.

In 1644 a similar action took place over the same ground when Colonel Sands and his Parliamentarians held the then rebuilt bridge and the road beyond for a considerable amount of time. Brotherton Marsh on the north bank of the Aire was then, and up to the first Ordnance Survey subject to flooding, the only causeway being the road from the bridge past Brotherton village nearby. Sir Henry Slingsby, a Royalist, remarked that they 'had to fight for ground to fight upon' until, through gaps and disadvantage, they drove the Parliamentarians from their position.[9] In 1461 the Yorkists probably did not even get across the River Aire to fight, or, if they did, they must have faced similar disadvantages in the marshes against the Lancastrians. They certainly incurred heavy casualties trying to dislodge Clifford from the bridge and many were drowned on both sides. The Earl of Warwick was shot in the leg by a chance arrow, according to William

Gregory, in what may have been one of many vain sallies across the narrow defile in a battle in which the larger force was typically held up by the smaller only as long as the manpower lasted.

According to Benet's Chronicle, Edward fought on foot at Ferrybridge, proving that desperate measures had to be employed to withstand the attacks by Lord Clifford's men across the makeshift bridge.[10] Finally the Yorkists probably decided they were losing too many men and, not wanting two disasters in the same day, according to Hall, Edward called for Fauconberg, Blount and Horne with the vaward to threaten Clifford's flank via Castleford. Informed of this, or actually after fighting their way out of this Yorkist flank attack, Clifford wisely decided to beat the retreat on a job well done, back to the main Lancastrian army, before his men were totally wiped out.

The Death of Lord Clifford

If we suppose that these events occurred during the morning of 28 March, the attack on the Lancastrians beginning at first light after the Fitzwalter débâcle in the early hours, then this gives ample time for the first assaults on Ferrybridge, a Fauconberg flank march via Castleford's bridge 3 miles away and then a simultaneous retreat by Clifford and advance by the Yorkist vaward up the Towton road before nightfall. Unfortunately neither Clifford nor his men ever reached the Lancastrian lines, because the Yorkist vaward's mounted contingent, always at their heels, cut them off and destroyed them, almost to a man, in sight of their own troops.

Edward Hall was the only one with information on this episode, and, to make matters worse, the other chroniclers were, predictably, either indecisive about the location of Clifford's death or placed his name among the long list of Lancastrian dead after the battle of Towton. But the 'Flower of Craven's' near annihilation is more important than the means or location of its commander's death, as now it left the Lancastrians deprived of one of their most valued captains. Hall gives the details of 'The Butcher's' last moments when Clifford's men

met with some that they looked not for, and were attrapped before they were aware. For the Lord Clifford, either from heat or pain, put off his gorget [armoured neck protection], was suddenly hit by an arrow, as some say, without a head and was stricken in the throat, and incontinent rendered his spirit. And the Earl of Westmorland's brother [John Neville] and all his company almost were slain, at a place called Dintingdale, not far from Towton.[11]

Dintingdale is a shallow valley that crosses the Ferrybridge–Tadcaster road to Towton below the plateau where the massive Lancastrian army was encamped. Earlier I mentioned Hall's possible 'comparisons' between some of the Lancastrian nobles. Could this clash of personalities have been the reason why Clifford was not reinforced as dusk was falling on 28 March? Clearly it seems that he was not offered any help from his Lancastrian friends on the plateau. Was there in fact dissension in the Lancastrian ranks after all, with leading magnates jockeying for position in the face of the enemy? It is hard to believe that Lancastrian scouts would not have been fanned out to warn the Duke of Somerset of a Yorkist approach, but where were they when one of the more illustrious and valuable Lancastrian commanders was being ambushed and killed at Dintingdale only 2½ miles from Towton?

Various reasons could account for this baffling event, such as a surprise attack in the dark on Clifford by the Yorkist mounted archers, who were by this time well up the road from Ferrybridge, although a chance arrow in the dark is hard to believe. Visibility may have been impaired – we know that the weather was bitterly cold, with snow in the offing the next day – so could the Lancastrians actually see Dintingdale from their position? A walk south on the battlefield today offers no sight of the valley in question until the triangulation point is reached beside the hawthorn tree at 168 feet, and, if the Lancastrians were encamped in and around Towton on the 28 March, the question is academic. If, alternatively, the Lancastrian camp was above Saxton, for instance near the triangulation point, or on Whitehill Fields, Somerset's troops would have had a grandstand view of Cifford's death. We can discard this theory of the same place providing both the viewpoint and in fact a battle position by asking ourselves whether the Lancastrian soldiers would have accepted watching Clifford and his men, gladiator-like, taking on the Yorkist mounted archers. This is very doubtful indeed given the damage it would have done to their morale.

The plain fact is that the Lancastrians may not have seen the Dintingdale skirmish at all, or, knowing of Clifford's predicament, wisely decided not to sally out into what might have been the whole oncoming Yorkist army, thus quitting the high ground and thereby disclosing their prepared position for the sake of a few hundred men. These were harsh times indeed, but no different from many other situations in military history.

What does come out of this discussion, however, is that the Lancastrian army must have been encamped in the village of Towton or immediately south of it on 28 March, with the usual pickets using the plateau's edge above Dintingdale like a castle wall to survey the land beyond. They may have reported back to Somerset, Northumberland or Exeter, telling of Clifford's entrapment; they may even have attempted to help the surrounded Lancastrians in vain. Whatever the scenario, through history's half-light it is apparent that Somerset and his advisers kept their ground, and another Clifford's blood stained a Wars of the Roses battlefield even before the main contest had begun.

Meanwhile at Ferrybridge, according to Jean de Waurin, the Yorkists, seeing Lord Clifford in flight, 'took the bridge, and all the army went over it the same night'.[12] During the advance, Yorkist bodies may have been cleared from the field, although, apart from the nobles, it is doubtful that burials could have been carried out on a large scale given the bad weather, the marshy land and King Edward's urgency to come to grips with the enemy. C. Forrest in describing Brotherton Marsh mentioned that 'Human skeletons, ancient armour and other relics of civil warfare have been frequently found there, and should the marsh ever be under the plough, many more such relics will certainly be turned up.'[13] However, Forrest was not certain whether the artifacts found were from the 1644 or 1461 engagements.

On the same topic, in *Archaeologia* Vol. IX, there is an interesting passage that speculates about the last resting place of at least one of the Yorkist lords near the battlefield. It reads:

> There was found in digging a grave in Brotherton churchyard, May 21st 1781, a chalice, very much mutilated, and its lid, a spur and parts of armour. These most probably belonged to one of the lords slain at Ferrybridge before the battle of Towton, on Saturday 28th March 1461. It was usual to inter the lords who fell in this contest near the place where they were slain, and it is probable that the chalice, spur and armour might belong to Lord Fitzwalter.[14]

Forrest's theory about these archaeological finds is that two ancient graves, one of a warrior and the other of an ecclesiastic, were invaded by the 1781 grave when it was dug and mistaken for one. Thus the story and the legend has been perpetuated, but unfortunately cannot be proven, especially since we have none of the remains surviving to date them.

The March to the Battlefield

On the eve of Palm Sunday 1461, Edward's army struggled northward from Ferrybridge. It is not clear whether the Duke of Norfolk had at last arrived at Pontefract by this time, but, judging by events the next day, there still seemed to be a serious delay. Some authorities deduce that John Mowbray was sick at Pontefract and sent his troops over the bridge after it had been strengthened on 29 March to arrive at Towton in the late afternoon of Palm Sunday. I for one think that Norfolk was always a day's march behind the main Yorkist army and had difficulties on the road north. Norfolk's men could have been dragging guns with them, slowing the pace, as I find it impossible to believe that Edward had not secured some artillery from London for his campaign. Being the rearward of the army, this may have called for drastic measures by Mowbray like their eventual abandonment in favour of speed, as there is no archaeological evidence to date of any artillery being used at the battle of Towton. Ferrybridge would also have been an excellent place to use such arms had they been available. Alternatively the Duke of Norfolk may have had trouble mustering troops, and, if he was indeed ill and absent from recruiting drives (he died later in the year on 6 November), this could have accounted for untold problems when he was attempting to secure his contingent's loyalties. Extending this theory further, if Norfolk was at Towton on Palm Sunday and ill, it is unlikely that he took part in the battle – a sick man would never have survived such a strength-sapping ordeal, especially a noble in armour-plate.

After the battle of Ferrybridge, the vaward, mainward and rearward of Edward's army were separated. Fauconberg with the vaward, after crossing the River Aire at Castleford, may have advanced up the Roman road to Hook Moor, below Aberford, and turned sharp right towards the abandoned medieval village of Lead, and Saxton beyond. But it is more likely that, because they were ordered to take Lord Clifford in the flank at Ferrybridge, the vaward chased the 'Flower of Craven' up the Tadcaster road where some of them, presumably the mounted archers, closed on Clifford later in the day. Edward pressed on after Fauconberg and advanced on Sherburn-in-Elmet, the next main town on the road north.

There is high ground above Saxton to the south-east, bordering Dintingdale and the north-west towards Lead, therefore it is possible that some of the Yorkist vaward, after their skirmish with Clifford, pitched what camps they had with them along this ridge and in the main village of Saxton. Jean de Waurin tells of the plight of the Yorkists, not forgetting the Lancastrians, on that cold Palm Sunday eve as Edward's strung-out forces struggled to link up with each other. 'It was so cold', Waurin reported, 'with snow and ice, that it was pitiful to see men and horses suffer, especially as they were badly fed.'[15]

Many men must have died of exposure in such conditions as there is no mention of cover or tents. The Yorkist baggage train was almost certainly still on the road carrying these basic requirements, especially food, which, judging by the the above extract, was in short supply in Edward's large army, at least. Indeed the Yorkist wagons may not have even yet crossed Ferrybridge. Prime billets would have been taken by the nobles, as the villagers in the area would probably have been long gone – perhaps some of them had already been recruited by the Lancastrians. All things considered, young Edward, with a seriously undernourished force-marched army under his command, must have wondered about his fate and his earlier decision to be judged by God in battle, now that the main event was approaching. Short of his religious beliefs, his thirst for revenge and the prize of the crown of England, Edward must have been a very rare individual indeed if he did not experience some doubts about the imminent battle. Being without the Duke of Norfolk's contingents must have weighed heavily on his mind, but it is difficult to imagine what he could have done differently to effect a meeting with his East Anglian foot-slogging allies, because he had been drawn on unpredictably like a magnet by the Lancastrians ever since he set foot in Yorkshire. After being harassed by them at Ferrybridge he again pushed on without the Duke of Norfolk, possibly leaving word of his departure at Pontefract or, more likely, sending word to John Mowbray to meet him the following day somewhere up the Tadcaster road where he would endeavour to engage the enemy.

The Yorkist vaward and the main Lancastrian army would most probably have been very close to each other across what would later become Towton battlefield. Before dawn, several isolated skirmishes may have occurred, as Hearne's Fragment recorded that there was some fighting during the night. However, it is highly unlikely that the two main armies fought at four o'clock in the afternoon through until the following morning, as he described. Large-scale medieval battles were never fought at night, by the light of fires or torches, as one antiquary would have us believe.

Of the two armies, the Yorkists must have been the worst for wear from the day's events: some soldiers would have been tired from marching, others may have been nursing wounds from Ferrybridge, and, even if still fit, they may not have relished the thought of fighting the next day with their injuries. Most men would have been wrapped in cloaks huddled around fires, cursing the Lancastrians for their present predicament. Only the chivalrous, such as Edward and the lords under his command, would have thought of religious vigil through prayer as their solace. The unblooded in both armies would have been apprehensive and fearful. Some of these may have deserted under cover of darkness beneath the grizzled veterans noses who talked of the French, feats of arms and loot. All, except the nobles, would have preferred not to fight a battle at all, unless they were a very remarkable breed indeed, and most wished only to fulfil their obligation to their captain or lord, with as little blood spilling as possible.

The Lancastrians, tented and secure around Towton, had already hit the Yorkists hard at the cost of Lord Clifford's life, and they must have felt very confident of victory the next day, if still suffering, like the Yorkists, from the effects of the harsh weather. At the risk of making the obvious comparison of the night before the battle of Agincourt, in this understandably parallel situation of the forced marched, unfed, bedraggled underdog versus the overconfident, rested and fresh 'enemy', are there perhaps any greater comparisons to be made in view of events so far and the manifestations in the next day's battle?

In the main, the Lancastrians were very unfortunate to have so many peers of the realm in their ranks in respect of affecting the most important factor in an army's make up – unity. This, when all else failed, was the common bond with which to repair uncertainty and fear in the face of a bleak turn of events. In the Lancastrian army this aim may have been threatened by more than a dozen overmighty subjects and their 'affinities' rubbing shoulders and powerbroking for the honours of leading their contingents first into battle against the Yorkists. Useful amalgamations of 'all arms' units under one command may not have been possible under these circumstances. Add to this the fact that the nobles were out for the traditional Wars of the Roses rewards, then consequently competition became the governing factor in the tactics of the forthcoming battle. The resulting lack of communication must have been a frustrating worry for their commander-in-chief, the Duke of Somerset.

Two massive armies were now poised for a great test of skill and fortitude, never to be repeated on such a large scale on British soil in the medieval era, and in which nearly half of its participants would perish for one King of England or the other. As sentries were buffeted by the freezing early morning wind and men were given absolution for their sins, one can only wonder at these warriors' resolve to enter into the violent abyss of the day's battle.

FIVE

Bloody Meadows

There can be little doubt as to where the battle of Towton took place, as all of the historical sources and local legends point to the same general area. We are also lucky in the evidence of battlefield grave sites, which are, given the unusually large casualties, as far as we know to date, quite extensive in the proximities of both Towton and Saxton parishes. Other historically linked areas of the battlefield are also marked very precisely on the first Ordnance Survey maps. As for other less well-marked sites, more explanation is needed because the locality and the battle need to be evaluated together in view of the incomplete documentary evidence concerning this harrowing and bloody encounter.

Medieval England was primarily an agricultural country, though in later times harsh climatic regions turned to mainly pastoral farming and rural crafts. Consequently tradesmen in these areas relied on selling their goods in return for corn and supplies from the more productive parts of the country. Agricultural yields were low, which in turn brought hardship and, in some instances, famine. In the 1300s bubonic plague ravaged the country on several occasions and remained endemic throughout the later Middle Ages. However, small family farms that came through these hard times of uncertainty found themselves in a very strong position in that the rapidly expanding population of the earlier Middle Ages had been drastically cut and marginal land such as woods, moors and marshes that had previously been occupied reverted to waste because of these problems. The enterprising farmers who acquired these areas therefore became owners of vast tracts of land, and they ditched and hedged bigger fields, which thus became commonplace on the English landscape.

Towton battlefield stands on the magnesium limestone belt of North Yorkshire, and as such we can expect the district to have been very fertile in some areas, consequently bringing about an early start to this type of field system. Most portions of the battlefield were certainly open pasture land in

1461, but there is evidence that the fields of both Towton and Saxton were extending quite some way from the villages in this period. John Leland, who visited Yorkshire in 1558, recorded in his *Itinerary* that areas near the battlefield such as Aberford and Tadcaster were 'good high plain, corn ground' and 'corn ground and some wood',[1] which clearly indicates a trend in the area by the Tudor period, at least. Leland also described Towton and Saxton fields as extending quite some distance from the villages, judging by his route along the River Cock past the deserted medieval settlement of Lead. Thus we cannot assume that this part of Yorkshire was barren wilderness at the time of the battle, or overrun with forest. Instead the exposed battlefield plateau must have been chiefly pasture land with pockets of cultivation and areas of partly cleared woodland bordering the site. Ridge and furrow field systems together with ancient hedgerows and woodland have been identified on the battlefield, which adds support to this theory.

Towton, almost due north of Saxton, was probably a small insignificant hamlet on the road to Tadcaster, although there is evidence that there was a Towton Hall here even in the reign of Richard II. The old London road from Ferrybridge and Sherburn-in-Elmet ran through the village and turned left to ascend, then precipitously descend the northernmost edge of the battlefield plateau to what may have been a wooden bridge, or more likely, in 1461, a ford, over the River Cock. This main crossing has become known locally as the legendary 'Bridge of Bodies', due to the clogging up of the site by Lancastrian dead during the eventual rout from the battlefield. However, as will be seen later, it is more likely that there were several such human dams along the river's winding course after the battle, which would account for similar descriptions along its length.

In 1847 *The Field of The Battle of Towton* by Richard Brooke was read before the Society of Antiquaries of London. With reference to the absence of a bridge over the River Cock in 1461, Brooke cited Biondi's work, which tends to confirm the existence of a ford. Translated from old Italian, it contains this information that, after the battle,

> Those who remained alive [the Lancastrians], took the road for the bridge at Tadcaster, but being unable to reach it, and believing a small river called Cock to be fordable, the greater part were drowned therein. It is constantly affirmed, that those who survived, passed over, treading on the dead bodies of the sufferers, and the water of this stream, and of

the River Wharfe, into which it empties itself, were coloured in a manner to appear as pure blood.[2]

As indicated in this passage, the River Cock flows northwards towards Tadcaster and meets the River Wharfe, but upstream, south of the 'Bridge of Bodies', it snakes 'S'-like along the western edge of Towton battlefield, past Cocksford, another possible local crossing place, Renshaw Wood and Castle Hill Wood. The river bulges menacingly into the battlefield plateau between these two woods and beckons the 'funnel' of Towton Dale and the legendary Bloody Meadow to its banks. All of this water was, and remains, bordered to the west by gently rising water-meadows, but, to the east, precipitous slopes rise to 150 feet in almost as many paces, and eventually climb onto the battlefield itself. All along the river's tortuous course it is the same story until, after circumnavigating Castle Hill and three mysterious tumuli, the river bubbles past St Mary's church at Lead in the much flatter surroundings, in comparison, near The Crooked Billet public house.

As described earlier, some of the Yorkist vaward commanders, in securing prime billets on the night of 28 March, may have occupied the Lead area. Parallel to Saxton and to the west of it, the now deserted medieval village, once owned by the Tyas and Skargill families, could have been the location of a Neville camp before the battle, possibly even the site of the Earl of Warwick's bivouac. Leland, in his Yorkshire *Itinerary*, mentioned while passing Lead that some buildings were still in existence then:

> Then by much turning to Lead, a hamlet, were Skargill had a fair manor place of timber. Cock Beck after crookith by Saxton and Towton village fields, and goith into Wharfe river a mile beneath Tadcaster.[3]

Heraldic devices also point to a theory and, I might add, a local tradition that 'The Crooked Billet' was associated with The White Ragged Staff badge of the Earl of Warwick's troops, and thus a legend has developed. However, there is no proof of the suggestion that there was an inn at Lead in 1461, especially on the B1217 Hook Moor to Towton road, which was not a well-worn route from Watling Street in those days. To cast further doubt on this theory, we must also take into account that, in the fifteenth century, towns usually had inns rather than isolated northern trackways.

This then is the description of the western perimeter of the battlefield, using the River Cock as a sinister landmark of a very dangerous area to be avoided at all costs, tactically speaking, especially as it is assumed that the water-meadows were flooded at the bottom of the steep slopes bordering that side of the plateau on the day of the battle. However, historically speaking, have we any evidence to support the suggestion that this flooding actually occurred to such an extent on Palm Sunday 1461? Certainly none of the chronicles mention flooded rivers either at Towton or Tadcaster. We may imagine that, in an effort to make the heavy drownings that must certainly have occurred there during the mass Lancastrian rout more horrifying, antiquarians and historians may have exaggerated the issue to account for the high death tolls and head counts that they read about in the chronicles. Further, how, with such a fast-flowing river, so deep and in spate, did the whole Lancastrian army and their baggage train cross over the River Cock to encamp and eventually fight at Towton, unless by coincidence the river flooded just after they crossed? Let us also remember that this was the Lancastrians' only line of communication with the king and queen in York, and to have knowingly had such a threatening river at their backs forming an obstacle would have been decidedly foolish by any military standards. Holding the river at Tadcaster would have been a much better plan under these circumstances rather than crossing the River Cock to find there could be no retreat later.

At the beginning of Chapter One I quoted George Neville in his letter to Coppini, which clearly stated that the bridge at Tadcaster was broken down by the Lancastrians after they had crossed it. In discussing the bridge, river and ford aspects of the battle of Towton, I find this, too, very difficult to comprehend, unless the Lancastrians were so very confident of victory that they threw caution to the wind and resolved to go back and rebuild the bridge at Tadcaster to assist their triumphant entry into York after defeating the Yorkists. They may, of course, have been worried about deserters in the army and 'used' the rivers Wharfe and Cock as natural barriers to such behaviour, but this is very hard to believe given that this sort of action to stop runaways never occurred in similar situations in the Wars of the Roses. Where armies had a river at their backs, every attempt was made to keep bridges intact. In contrast, in retreat, bridges were better destroyed, and it is more logical that the Lancastrian fugitives from Towton sabotaged the bridge over the Wharfe in their retreat to protect themselves and the king, similar to the action taken by the Duke of York after the rout at Ludford in 1459.

Compared with the River Wharfe, the River Cock was only a tributary, but it must have been a veritable death trap without the exaggerations of Victorian romanticism. Steep-sided and, in parts, still very deep today, it is shallower than it would have been in 1461 because of gradual infill over the years. The unfortunate soldiers rushing in panic headlong down its vertical sides into its freezing watery grave must have thought this was the worst possible obstacle to encounter in their bid to stay alive. However, the River Wharfe was the more formidable barrier of the two, and consequently it was to play a major role in the battle of Towton during the Lancastrian rout from the field.

Today the eastern edge of Towton battlefield is bordered by the Tadcaster–Ferrybridge turnpike road, which for our purposes runs from Towton south, again following the contours of the battlefield plateau, past Saxton Grange to Dintingdale, Scarthingwell and eventually to Barkston Ash. This road is the continuation of the old London road through Towton from 'The Bridge of Bodies', and it is difficult to disprove its existence in 1461, although some historians have tried, claiming that from Barkston Ash the road turned left to Saxton and then followed Cotchers Lane over the battlefield plateau to meet the present B1217 to Towton. In accepting this theory it is difficult to understand the reason why the main road made this detour, when the more direct route north to Towton, Tadcaster and, more important, the fords over the River Cock was the eastern perimeter of the battlefield plateau. However, a local track through Dintingdale from Scarthingwell to Saxton and Lead was almost certainly in existence, although it would not have been a main thoroughfare in the medieval era, as it served a purpose in bisecting the angle of the two roads to Towton.

To the east of the Tadcaster–Ferrybridge turnpike and the battlefield there is descending, and in some places flat, mainly low-lying land with springs and water-meadows. In 1461 this was more than likely marshland in some areas for some considerable distance to Dintingdale and would have formed another formidable barrier with which to anchor and protect the flank of an army, although this feature in turn could also prevent movement for defenders and attackers alike. Dintingdale, as mentioned, is marked on most maps of the area, but pinpointing this elusive landmark is entirely fruitless in my opinion as the dale, most probably the whole valley from

Saxton to Scarthingwell across the southern edge of the battlefield, was undoubtedly named from a large tract of land that was in existence when Edward Hall wrote his chronicle in the 1500s, as he alone told of what happened to Lord Clifford on the eve of Palm Sunday. Another place cited as Lord Clifford's Dintingdale is the land between Scarthingwell and Barkston Ash, in particular the area marked by a derelict stone cross foundation plinth, commonly called 'The Leper Pot'.

This curiosity may once have supported an upright cross situated in the still visible hollowed-out block of limestone, and may in fact have been erected to commemorate Clifford's death there in 1461. Unfortunately neither local tradition nor chronicles support the theory, although I have to admit that this site of 'The Butcher's' death would account for Lancastrian scouts having not seen 'The Flower of Craven's' skirmish with the Yorkists from their picket lines. Further support for the existence of Lord Clifford's Cross at Barkston Ash is the fact that 'The Leper Pot' tradition is, in my opinion, very weak, even given that at one time Tadcaster had a colony for these diseased unfortunates nearby. It is very unlikely that these people would have travelled such a great distance, through Towton incidentally, to receive food for money out of a hollowed-out stone slab. That 'The Leper Pot' was a cross at some time, locating the position of Clifford's death exactly, rather than Dintingdale, which is such a large area of land, is an interesting concept.

We must, however, temper this idea with the stories of a possible grave pit containing the bodies of Lord Clifford, John Neville and others of their contingent near the present-day Dintingdale itself. In 1835 an 'amateur' excavation was carried out in the vicinity and a pit was dug close to the turnpike road. In it were found bones supposed to have been the remains of Lord Clifford, although how the antiquarians could have identified Clifford's body in particular is difficult to comprehend. Here, though, we have evidence of the existence of a burial pit of some kind, with remains of some sort, near the battle zone, thus contradictions regarding the Clifford Cross theory can be brought to bear, especially given that a Clifford family tradition states that 'The Butcher' was 'tumbled into a pit of promiscuous dead bodies after the battle of Towton'.[4] It is doubtful that men carried these bodies very far from their place of death after the preceding skirmish at Dintingdale.

To complete the battlefield 'triangle' encompassing the main killing fields of Palm Sunday 1461, the southern edge of the site is famous for the most tangible, visual and time-evoking edifice of the Towton battlefield story. The dark, battered and mysterious tomb of Lord Dacre bears silent witness to the fact that this medieval battle was certainly about death at its most basic and violent level, in that not only is this noble interred in the Saxton village churchyard of All Saints, but also with him are hundreds of others of lesser degree. The trench graves recorded here in various topographic accounts must contain a veritable human foundation of bones to the north side of the parish church running east to west, because remains have been continually unearthed here down the centuries.

Visible as regular undulations in the ground, and identified by antiquaries as belonging to the victims of the battle, the graves represent the burial mounds of those bodies that found consecrated ground in contrast to the more unfortunate who were interred on the field of battle. John Leland recorded the existence of graves here first, and in his *Itinerary* wrote that 'In the churchyard were many of the bones of men that were killed at Palmsunday Field buried'.[5] One of Leland's contemporaries in the local Hungate family added to the 'fellowship of death' when he 'gathered a great number of the bones from the fields and caused them to be buried in Saxton churchyard'.[6] The Hungates were lords of the manor at Saxton and the shallow graves on the battlefield, of which more later, may have prompted this venerable man to reinter some exposed bones of Yorkist and Lancastrians alike when the plough was used to extend Saxton village's fields in the Tudor period. Some of these remains are said to have been unearthed in Saxton churchyard during the 1840s, lying about four feet below the surface, and the bones exposed were thought to have been 'either young, or in the prime of life because the skulls were remarkable for their soundness and excellence of teeth'.[7] These excavations, however, were possibly the original Yorkist trench graves on the north side of Saxton Church and not the Hungate collection of bones, which may have been stumbled across by gravediggers over the years.

John Neville, mistaken by Leland in his *Itinerary* for the Earl of Westmorland (who was Neville's brother), is also said to have been buried within Saxton Church by the fathers the Tudor traveller interviewed in the village in 1585. Given this fact, then, are we to assume that Lord Clifford, as Neville's kinsman and partner in death at Dintingdale, is also buried somewhere at All Saints along with his Lancastrian friend and ally Lord Dacre? Someone obviously took the time to make sure that at least some of the Lancastrians had decent burials, and indeed were recorded, in contrast with the Yorkist unlettered dead of which no names, memorials or records survive.

To explain this we must first take into account that this part of Yorkshire was Lancastrian country in those days, and therefore we must assume the obvious in that some Yorkists were most certainly interred in Saxton churchyard. (Some of their rough-hewn stone gravestones may have been used to build the church tower.) Later, however, the prominent Lancastrians were also given burials here when the Yorkists had moved on after the battle. After all, even the bells in the tower of Saxton Church are old enough to commemorate a Lancastrian loss rather than a Yorkist victory. These date from the late medieval period and still function perfectly in their original housing, despite their age. The donor of one of them, William Sallay, who died in 1492, had an inscription cast on his that says it all when a lost cause is kept alive by the faithful. The inscription reads:

Willeimus Sallay armiger de Saxton me fecit fieri Sancta Margarita ora pro nobis.[8] (William Sallay Lord of Saxton caused me to be made, St Margaret pray for us.)

In view of this, either William Sallay or the Hungates, both lords of the manor of Saxton, are partly connected with Lord Dacre's tomb, along with the noble's family, due to their outwardly staunch Lancastrian sympathies. It is doubtful that the Yorkist regime was the least bit concerned with burying such Lancastrian traitors as Lord Dacre, who was, along with his allies, attained by Edward IV in 1461.

Furthering pro-Lancastrian sentiment, Lord Dacre's 'meane tomb' also has a patriotic inscription that reads:

Here lies Randolf, Lord of Dacre and Gilsland, a true knight, valiant in battle in the service of King Henry VI, who died on Palm Sunday, 29 March 1461, on whose soul may God have mercy, Amen.[9]

The tomb, about 2½ feet high, displaying Lord Dacre's heraldic achievements on its sides, is today in a sad state of repair. Wrenched open, defaced and broken in two pieces by the curious and the disrespectful, it is now 'protected' by iron rails. In 1749 the tomb had metal clamps around it, which were broken to inter a Mr Gascoigne in the same place and while digging this grave an amazing, but sadly amateur, discovery was made. Lord Dacre's skeleton was discovered upright in a standing position. Even more mysterious is that, in 1861, adjacent to the tomb, the ground was disturbed once again, and in digging another grave the skull of a horse (now in the British Museum) and its vertebrae were unearthed, extending into the Dacre tomb, thus confirming a legend that both the noble and his faithful courser were buried together. This strange mode of burial is, to my knowledge, unique to medieval history in that, if one can explain the standing burial as being of Celtic origin, what then is Dacre of Gilsland doing buried with his horse? And is the horse also upright – as some have claimed – of the same date and actually the noble's own war horse that he brought to the battle of Towton? A great mystery indeed, but the truth, as always, will be a far stranger story.

Raising still more questions over the years about this bizzare Craven limestone tomb is the fact that the inscription on its lid is partly incomplete because of a damaged section, namely the missing portion containing Dacre's title. One of the original transcripts of Dacre's tomb has the lord being 'of Greystock' and not of Gilsland. However, because both titles became one and the same when the barony of Greystock united with that of Dacre of Gilsland by marriage, the argument the Victorian antiquarians perpetuated is irrelevant and need never have caused confusion.

Topography of the Battlefield

So to the battlefield of Towton itself, lying in the confines of the triangle of roads and features so far described, and on top of a plateau bordered by varying degrees of slopes and gullys. It was on this high ground that the battle was contested. There is no doubt of this, as, first, the position is corroborated by the simple fact that the features investigated so far, such as river, village and marsh, provide a totally unsuitable terrain for fighting a large-scale medieval battle. Space is the crucial factor here, and was to become a vital prerequisite and, eventually, a major concern to both armies, when the main trial of strength was underway in the early afternoon of Palm Sunday. Second, the battlefield, unlike some others, is marked quite precisely by other well-documented features such as grave pits, 'red pieces' (bloody meadows) and consistent legends and traditions.

In the principal areas of conflict the battle zone is 100 ft above the surrounding land (150 ft above sea level) and in general consists of the high ground bisected east to west with a low valley known as Towton Dale to the west and North Acres to the east. On the western side of this depression in the land, Towton Dale 'funnels' steeply into the River Cock valley in which Bloody Meadow shares the dale's precipitous descent. Bloody Meadow contained five gravepits that John Leland saw when he visited the site in the Tudor period, and he related them in his *Itinerary* to the removal of bones and their reinterment in consecrated ground by the Hungates. The full passage reads:

In the churchyard were many of the bones of men that were killed at Palmsunday Field buried. They lay afore in 5 pits, yet appearing half a mile by north in Saxton fields.[10]

These five mounds were visible fifty years before Dr Whittaker published his account of the battle of Towton in *Leodis and Elmete* in 1816. In his book, Whittaker stated that he saw little trace of the grave site then, which is surprising because some accounts of a later date contradict this statement. However, in the Field of the White and Red Rose, also alluded to as Bloody Meadow, Richard Brooke, who visited the battlefield between 1848 and 1856, claims that:

The large meadow is remarkable for producing rich rank grass, and also for three or four extensive irregularly shaped patches of very small wild dwarf rose bushes, which I was told, were both red and white.[11]

These patches of the Towton Rose (*Rosa spinosissima*), now almost an extinct plant species in the area, were on the left-hand side of the B1217 road to Towton as it begins to descend into the depression across the battlefield, and are in my view evidence of disturbed ground cover probably on four of the five grave sites described by Leland in 1558.

Bloody Meadow was to become the bloodiest of the bloody meadows on Towton battlefield. However, in view of the resulting rout, it is more than likely that this whole valley at the western end of the plateau's depression was by the the end of the battle so littered with corpses that it is perhaps irrelevant to mark one meadow as being the most horrifying. More important is the fact that this forward slope may have been the best place to bury the dead because of the fact that some, if not the majority of the battlefield, is situated on limestone and in parts the soil is not very deep for large graves to have been dug. We must therefore not expect the grave sites to be in the areas of the greatest slaughter, especially as the limestone is only two feet below the surface in some places.

Evidence of more burials existed in the middle of the plateau's depression looking north towards Towton, on the opposite ridge of the battlefield, at a site known as The Graves. According to the Harleian Manuscript (MS 795) there were

Certain deep trenches overgrown with bushes and briers containing 19 yards in breadth and 32 yards in length in Towton field, a bowshot on the left hand in the way betwixt Saxton and Towton, half a mile short of Towton.[12]

According to some sources this was a raised enclosure, the borders of which are still visible. However, the plough has been here over the centuries and levelled the land, so that nothing remains of these extensive trench graves today except for the perimeter, which is wound in and out of by tractors, almost as if there still is a blueprint on the land over five hundred years later.

The tract of land in front of this site and extending a considerable distance west to the B1217 road and east to the Tadcaster–Ferrybridge turnpike is called North Acres. It was somewhere in these fields that Lord Dacre was supposed to have been killed at the height of the battle of Towton. The spot is unmarked, but a legend, recorded by Glover in his visitation, has it that 'the Lord of Dacres was slain in North Acres'[13] by a bowman who shot at him from out of a bur tree after the unfortunate noble had unclasped his helmet to drink a cup of wine. The tree, featured on Ordnance Survey maps, is precisely marked almost opposite The Graves in the hollow of the depression, 250 yards from the B1217 on the right-hand side of the road to Towton. Several overgrown bur elder tree stumps are still visible in this high bank, which may once have been an ancient hedgerow, and, although nothing remains today of the Dacre bur tree itself, the tradition, picked up by Glover when he conducted his visitation in 1585, serves a purpose in pinpointing the battle zone as well as perpetuating an interesting legend.

At the eastern end of North Acres the depression dips to the Tadcaster–Ferrybridge road, Saxton Grange and the flatlands beyond. This descent is not a precipitous drop like Towton Dale in the west, but, at the hawthorn tree and the triangulation point above North Acres, the land does fall away very quickly, similar to the inclines in the west. At a height of over 150 ft the hawthorn tree is in a very commanding position, and in fact there is no better view of the battlefield and the surrounding country. This must have been a very similar vantage point when the battle of Towton was fought, and one to occupy if possible once the engagement had begun. However, opposite this area, on the other ridge across the depression, was also a very commanding position, which in parts is almost as elevated.

On this site, where the battle cross now stands, the land is also 150 ft high and offers just as good a vantage point looking south as the hawthorn tree does north. There is a theory that this 'Battle Cross Ridge', containing The Graves, was in 1461 very much more extended towards the turnpike road, level with Saxton Grange, and, due to the levelling effects of the plough over the years, Towton Dale and North Acres combined may originally have been much deeper and more of a valley than the hollow depression that exists today. This may be true, but, as it turns out, any theory can be accepted if the need is there, and, as will be seen later, this 'Battle Cross Ridge' high ground does not present a serious argument when describing a 'good position' on which to deploy an army when other important factors are considered as well.

The battle of Towton memorial cross, namely the carved section at the top of the fairly modern obelisk, is very old, but its history is uncertain. Because of this, various stories have been attributed to it over the years, all of which are credible explanations of its origin. One antiquarian's book (W. Wheater, *History of Sherburn and Cawood*) has the battered carving sketched in a hedge bottom captioned 'Lord Dacre's Cross'. Others would have it that the cross could have been part of Lord Clifford's monument linked with 'The Leper Pot' at Barkston Ash. My theory, which is not unique, is that the cross may have come from the unfinished chapel commissioned by Richard III at Towton 'In token of prayer' and for the souls of 'the men slain at Palmsunday Field'.[14]

This chantry chapel was situated on the rising ground to the north of Towton Hall, where many more gravepits are to be found, as one might expect. Again it comes as no surprise to learn that some of these trenches, too, have been excavated by the curious, and sadly not well recorded for posterity. Before Francis Drake published his *Eboracum* in 1736, he and two others went to see a fresh grave opened, which may have been near Towton Hall. Among vast quantities of bones they found some arrow piles, pieces of broken swords and five groat pieces of Henry IV, V and VI. These were laid together, close to a thigh-bone, which made them conjecture that there had not been time to strip the bodies before they were tossed into the pit.[15] In view of events on Palm Sunday 1461, and immediately afterwards, the assumption that the coins were missed by looters is also a reasonable theory in view of the fact that only small burial parties could have been organized to dig the vast number of graves needed for the Towton dead. Therefore we must not attach too much importance on speed to get the dead buried, especially when the bodies were spread over an area 6 miles long by 3 miles wide. The clearing-up operation must also have been hampered by the bad weather because, according to George Neville, the dead were left in the fields for several days without burial.

Hundreds, perhaps thousands, were buried near the unfinished chapel, the full extent of which came to light when the cellars of Towton Hall were extended to meet a solid wall of human skeletons in the late 1700s. Excavations conducted by Bradford University in July 1996 also uncovered a substantial burial pit which was thoroughly investigated and recorded. Because of this large graveyard it is not surprising that this area of Towton village was selected to raise a chapel to the dead, and perhaps the battle cross originally marked the site of these graves. Richard III, who commissioned the chantry, would have known, but unfortunately he was to join the Wars of the Roses' death toll on Bosworth Field in 1485, thus the chapel was never finished and in time fell into ruin, and in the end disappeared altogether.

Bordering the battlefield's western edge along its length, except for the 'funnel' of Towton Dale and Bloody Meadow, are wooded areas. Renshaw Wood, extending northwards from Towton Dale along the course of the River Cock and the battlefield plateau, spreads further than the Bridge of Bodies, while to the west of Bloody Meadow, Castle Hill Wood covers the bluff overlooking a bulge in the River Cock and extends east onto the southern plateau. In 1461 these two woods must have extended a lot further eastwards onto the battlefield, but, judging by the site and confirmed by the areas we have investigated already, not so far as to have caused serious positional problems for the two armies. In fact there must have been a great many trees and bushes dotted all around the battlefield heathland, probably windswept and bent due to the plateau's exposed outlook, and like Lord Dacre's bur or elderberry tree in appearance.

The all-important point to remember here about the battle site, aside from its bordering features, is the width available to both armies on the plateau and, because of it, the effect on the masses of men thrown into combat. At this stage it is sufficient to say that, of the two elevations split by the depression, the southern ridge was, and is more so today, the most spacious in width, extending some 1,500 yards. But of this, only 1,000 yards face the parallel northern ridge, leading us to assume that at some time during the battle this expanse, containing Bloody Meadow, the Field of the White and Red Rose, Towton Dale, the bur tree and North Acres, was the main killing fields of Towton battlefield. I say 'main' because, as will become apparent when assessing the movements of this large contest, we can definitely not say that the depression was the only area of conflict, nor deaths for that matter, because there was ample space for manoeuvring and recoil for both armies on the plateau.

Taking this point further, and possibly pinpointing more gravesites in the process, we must also take into account the three tumuli at the base of a very steep descent to the south-east of Castle Hill Wood, which have not been under the plough. If these mounds are what they seem, they have not been fully recorded by antiquarians or travellers in describing the topography of the battlefield, which is, given their size, rather strange. However, because of their concealed location, it is possible that they were missed by all but the Victorians, who mention them briefly but understandably placed more emphasis on the accepted points of interest when describing the battlefield. In October 1993 I, together with the Towton Battlefield Society and archaeologist Andrew Green, carried out preliminary excavations on two of the three mounds, to determine exactly what they were, but no human remains or artifacts from the battle were found. However, the River Cock flooded the excavations at a depth of approximately two feet below ground level, which leads us to speculate what could be below this depth in very dry weather. As mentioned earlier, grave sites are important in identifying the general area of the battle of Towton, but a more important point to remember about the movements of the armies on the day is the 1,000 yards available from the battlefield depression to the edge of the southern plateau. Even without the graves to mark this distance, we may conclude, taking into account all of the 'red pieces' and legends linked with Palmsunday Field, that the battle of Towton was fought in a very circumscribed area of just over half a square mile, not including the rout, which according to the Bishop of Exeter was mercilessly followed up twelve times this distance towards Tadcaster.

Studying the chronicles and attainder documents, we can further pinpoint the above location of the battle of Towton as, first, Edward Hall indicated that 'Both hosts approached each other in a plain field between the villages of Towton and Saxton'.[16] Second, John Leland's *Itinerary* recorded that 'This field was as much fought in Saxton parish as in Towton, yet it beareth the name of Towton'.[17] And third, in eking out the bad blood of the then rebel Lancastrians, King Edward stated that the attainted Lancastrians traitorously rebelled against his person 'On Sunday called commonly Palm Sunday, the 29th day of March . . . in a field between the towns of Sherburn-in-Elmet and Tadcaster' and in 'Saxtonfield and Towtonfield'.[18]

Prelude to the Battle

More concerning the general area and the manoeuvres before the battle, the chronicle written by Jean de Waurin gives some interesting, though uncorroborated, evidence that could be linked more to the importance of the two towns of Sherburn-in-Elmet and Tadcaster rather than the villages of Towton and Saxton. Substantiating the author's claims is the key point here, but considering the timing of the actions at Towton and Ferrybridge, plus the logistical necessities of Edward's army on the march, we may be able to draw some new conclusions with Waurin's unusual prelude to the battle. After spending a bitterly cold night somewhere across the River Aire after the battle of Ferrybridge, the Yorkist army was brought news of the Lancastrian position by its scouts on Palm Sunday morning, the day of the battle of Towton:

When the Earl of March [Edward IV] and his lords were told that King Henry was nearby in the fields they rejoiced, for they wished for nothing more but to fight him. The earl called for his captains and told them to put their men in formation and to take their positions before the enemy came too close. And so it was he organized his battles, and he sent some men to look around the area because they were only 4 miles from the enemy. They did not go very far before they spotted the reconnaissance party from the enemy, and they quickly returned to the Earl of March to tell him that they had seen large numbers of men at arms in the fields and the banners of King Henry. They told him how the enemy was manoeuvering and their position, and when the earl was warned of this he went to his cavalry, which he had positioned on the wing, and said to them 'My children, I pray today that we shall be good and loyal to each other because we are fighting for a good cause!' After they had all echoed this thought a messenger came to tell the earl that the vaward troops of the king had started to move forward and the earl went back to place himself behind his banners.[19]

According to this the Lancastrians were already well advanced from Tadcaster early on Palm Sunday morning and actually 'in the fields' when the Yorkists, 4 miles distant, broke camp. This, then, is a clear indication that both armies were marching on the day of the battle. However, given the battlefield plateau position, a chance encounter is misleading in that the battle of Towton was almost certainly a set piece action, given the size of the armies, and because of the amount of reconnaissance that was obviously going on. Part of the Yorkist vaward was, after all, very close to Towton battlefield because of its skirmish with Lord Clifford late the previous day. It was probably this advanced 'battle' that sent reports back to Edward of Lancastrian troop movements during the morning of 29 March.

More of an interesting tactical alternative to existing theories about the battle of Towton is that the apparent reconnoitring was still in full swing early on Palm Sunday morning. Because of Waurin's evidence of a Yorkist encampment soon after the battle of Ferrybridge, this could also lead us to consider a very credible logistical alternative.

Edward IV's bill of attainder maintains that the main towns of Tadcaster and Sherburn-in-Elmet were far more important localities and logistical 'staging posts' than the two hamlets of Towton and Saxton on the road north. Therefore, if the Yorkists were encamped at Sherburn-in-Elmet (4 miles from Towton) soon after the battle of Ferrybridge, and the Lancastrians were similarly encamped at Tadcaster en route to Towton, the two towns would have provided far superior billeting and command positions for both armies the night before the battle than the two hamlets of Saxton and Towton.

If we accept this tactical and logistical evidence we must rethink existing theories that the 'whole' of the Yorkist army was encamped at Saxton and Lead before the battle of Towton. It seems obvious that the Yorkist mainward was still marching up the Tadcaster–Ferrybridge road on the morning of 29 March to effect a meeting with its vaward at Saxton. It has always been a mystery to me how the separated Yorkist vaward and mainward arrived together at Saxton and Lead the night before the battle of Towton. If the reader accepts Waurin's account as being plausible, considering all the above tactical and logistical evidence, here is one new alternative to consider.

More information about the predominance of Towton village over Saxton in respect of the battle's name is supplied in Hearne's Fragment, one of three fifteenth-century chronicles printed by him in 1719, and Polydore Vergil's *History of England*. These sources have the Yorkists advancing on Towton and not Saxton, but, considering the accepted Lancastrian presence in this area, it is perhaps not surprising considering that Towton was on the main road north and Saxton was just situated on a local track. However, the name of Towton has stuck with the battle, even though the action was mostly fought in Saxton parish. Before this, documents of the period referred more to 'Palmsunday Field', 'York Field', 'the battle of Cockbridge' or even 'The Battle of Sherburn'. Such are the problems of documentary evidence of the period on this elusive encounter, and also a lesson not to take the words contained in such sources too literally as, in most cases, contradictions abound.

The battle of Palmsunday Field is not, however, in my opinion, about contradictions at all, but instead about alternatives for the reader to analyse and then make up his/her own mind about what really happened. Documentary evidence is sadly lacking, so-called reliable accounts lack detail and eyewitnesses are non-existent. How then can anyone judge what is the definitive story of what unfolded in the bloody meadows of Towton battlefield, without good detailed chroniclers to affirm what we would like to claim as undisputed fact, or what is supported by other so-called well documented engagements of the medieval era. Our only way forward in this instance is to support the facts and parallels with the tactical effects of weapons and armour, the terrain, archaeological finds and to apply logic. More important, we must apply what we have learned so far about the wars between York and Lancaster, the attitude of kings, nobles, retainers and levies to combat, and the physical and mental drain on the human body in such a horrific and violent situation. Then we may at least come close to what happened between Saxton and Towton, and marvel at what many have called the Pharsalia of England, after a very large battle which was fought at Pharsalia in Thessaly, where Pompey was decisively defeated by Julius Caesar in 48 BC. Towton has been likened to this chiefly by the Victorians.

SIX

Palmsunday Field

The northern party made them strong with spear and with shield,
On Palmsunday afternoon they met us in the field,
Within an hour they were right fayne to flee, and eke to yield,
Twenty seven thousand The Rose killed in the field,
Blessed be the time, that ever God spread that flower.[1]

T he Rose of Rouen' contains one of the many erroneous figures claiming how many men were killed on Palmsunday Field. Indeed, all of the chroniclers of the battle of Towton provide their readers with unbelievable figures, both in numbers of participants and the enormous death tolls incurred because of the apparent length and ferocity of the battle. Not surprisingly these estimates have long been the subject of much heated debate, causing modern theories of smaller estimates of participants and consequently proportionally lower death tolls to be superseded by theories of greater numbers to combat this modernist threat, as if some contest existed.

This daunting mathematical dilemma regarding whether approximately 10,000 to 100,000 soldiers took part in the battle of Towton, and whether up to 38,000 of these were left dead on the field, is, to say the least, a great problem to resolve with logical thinking. But to judge the truth from pure exaggeration in the chronicles is an even more frustrating task, and in the end it is anyone's guess who is trying to deceive whom with these calculations. In concluding armies of biblical proportions, chroniclers, in their often moralistic monastic way, elevated their benefactor king to greater heights of power and at the same time instilled God-like fear of their sovereign's wrath on his subjects and enemies. In giving the plague-like death tolls the author does exactly the same, and in George Neville's case, for instance, abhors the loss of English lives for his own end, taking an opportunity to sympathize with Papal Legate Coppini's machinations to support a less than popular crusade against the 'enemies of the Christian name'.[2] In short the chronicler makes the numbers work for a particular function. We all inherently tend to do the same, no matter how hard we try not to.

So how many men faced each other across the fields beneath the banners and standards of their captains at the battle of Towton? Was it the more usual armies of between approximately 5,000 and 10,000 men per side, or perhaps ten times that number, defying all logic and rationality?

Besides such musters of men undertaken, for instance, at Bridport through Commissions of Array, the only reliable recorded benchmark we can apply to assess how many soldiers a king and his 'loyal' nobility could raise in England, Scotland and the Marches at this time is the army that Edward IV took on his bloodless expedition to France in 1475. An army of nearly 12,000 men was raised in 1475 – a similar figure, as it happens, to King Henry's southern counties muster in 1457, of which Bridport was a part. Regionally, though, apart from this, we know that the leading nobles of the land each raised average retinues of 2,000 to 3,000 men on numerous occasions during the Wars of the Roses, because bills for payment still exist for cloth to make livery jackets and badges for their men. At the other end of the social scale a Westmorland squire such as Walter Strickland, who contracted with the Earl of Salisbury in 1452, could also muster a very respectable 300 armed men, comprising archers and billmen.

If we take all of this into account and apply these figures to the large number of peers in the Lancastrian army at Towton and the lesser proportion of magnates in the Yorkist force, the claims of such chroniclers as Edward Hall must be considered as unusually high, simply because each noble could not possibly have raised such vast numbers of men in the fifteenth century. Edward Hall gives his exact figure of 48,640 for the Yorkist army at Towton, using the pay roll as his source of information. He computes the Lancastrian army at 60,000. However, many in the army were paid who did not fight, such as secretaries, royal servants and councillors, plus the figure, always in a state of flux and mainly on the decrease because of deaths and desertions, would not have remained static indefinitely between the beginning and end of March 1461. So the apparent authority of Hall is also questionable, not to mention where the elusive payroll is today to verify his claims.

Greater figures than Hall's computations are very doubtful, while anything less than 12,000 men in either army is an insult to both the structure of Livery and Maintenance and Commissions of Array, not forgetting that foreign mercenaries, and Scottish and Welsh troops, were also available. The key point to remember here is that a great effort was made to muster all able-bodied men in the country for the Towton campaign through all recruitment methods possible. After all, the war was by this stage at its height – a conflict between north and south in some respects, and king against king, in which everyone had some sort of stake in the outcome. A.H. Burne in his *Battlefields of England* had an interesting theory on the subject of numbers at the battle of Towton, which warrants attention, purely because it represents a 'best estimate' per head of population. He states that:

> No one knows what the population [of England] was in 1461. *The Historical Geography of England before 1800* computes it as 4,688,000 about a century later. If we accept a conservative estimate of 3 and a half millions in 1461, with a fighting age of 15 to 40, we get something in the neighbourhood of 500,000 potential soldiers. If we allow that 75,000 took part in the battle [of Towton] that comes to 15% of the potential soldiers.[3]

Burne's 15 per cent computation led him to believe that the Yorkists fielded 36,000 men and the Lancastrians, being better supplied with peers, amassed 40,000 men, the largest amount of manpower ever assembled for a pitched battle on British soil. However, these sorts of figures have been challenged in respect of the very low fighting age of fifteen, for instance, and also the estimated population at the time.

To counter the first problem, let us not forget that the potential King of England, Edward IV, was only eighteen himself when at Towton and, for all his youthful years, commanded and took an active part in the battle, and towered over his subjects at 6 feet 3 inches tall. As Burne reminds us, Harry Hotspur commanded a successful assault on Berwick at the age of twelve, so it is not unreasonable to suggest, indeed it is more than likely to expect, far younger men than Edward IV in both sides at the battle of Towton. The endurance and fitness of such young men must have been a vital prerequisite for an efficient fighting force in the medieval slogging match that most battles inevitably became. Most of these troops would have been well versed in arms, especially the longbow, from an early age, so the reason for using their potential as soon as possible is self evident. If we need to extend Burne's theories even further, for example to an older fighting man, the veteran captain Lord Fauconberg was sixty at Towton. The inclusion of older men thus makes the total of potential soldiers even greater.

However, more serious arguments against Burne's figures can be brought to bear because, first, the population of England was probably a lot less in 1461 (possibly 2.2 million), and, second, the potential number of soldiers must have been already depleted by the wars, not only in casualties inflicted but also in the inability of the nobles to raise such large contingents time and time again. As explained earlier, it is not surprising that this whole subject of numbers involved in the battle of Towton is a quagmire of supposition. However, it would be wrong of me to disregard the issue and not to make a judgement myself, based on averages of men raised by the nobles for other engagements in the Wars of the Roses, available frontages, the duration of the battle, and, to verify the resulting figure, the all important casualties inflicted on the day. Hopefully, by assessing the above factors throughout this chapter, the figures below may prove that what an army 'looked like' in numbers, and how many casualties there 'appeared' to be after the battle, differed greatly from reality. It is perhaps not surprising that chroniclers' figures vary when describing such large numbers of men, as even witnesses to the battle of Towton must have had great difficulty quantifying the massive armies.

If the leading peers in both armies could raise an average of 2,000 to 3,000 men and the lords an average of 300 to 500, then we should, with the help of Edward IV's attainder and the later evidence of the nobles we know were at Towton, be able to calculate the average Lancastrian strength with some degree of accuracy. The Lancastrians had in their ranks five peers of the realm, eight lords and an impressive array of knights, which may have amounted to 20,000 men, according to the averages above. These were the retinues that formed the foundation of the army. To this we must add the town militias, who were recruited through Commissions of Array, such as the city of York, which sent 1,000 men to the battle. We must also make some allowance for foreign mercenaries. These additional troops may have accounted for at least 5,000 more men, thus the figure of 25,000 seems to me sensible for the Duke of Somerset's army.

Taking into account Edward's army of the Marches, recently engaged at

Mortimers Cross, and the Earl of Warwick's remnants from the second battle of St Albans, the Yorkist army must have numbered at least 15,000 at the start of the campaign when fully gathered in London with the southern shires. It may have been even larger, given that these southern counties could, and did on several occasions, muster far greater numbers of men compared with the north. However, the Yorkist march, the bad weather and the battle of Ferrybridge must have claimed a fair proportion of this figure. So, if we say that Edward, Warwick and Fauconberg's contingents once united at the beginning of the battle of Towton amounted to 20,000 men, with the Duke of Norfolk still on the road with 5,000 men, we cannot be too far away from the truth, given that the Lancastrians were superior to the Yorkists in strength. Let us not forget that almost all of the nobility of England was assembled for the battle of Towton, in contrast with the usual Wars of the Roses armies fielding relatively small turnouts of nobles, which when mustered amounted to numbers approaching around 5,000 men. It is possible, with the number of peers and their 'affinities' in both armies' ranks, that 5,000 armed men formed only part of one of the usual three divisions or 'battles' at Towton.

In accepting the above calculations can we support these figures with the horrifying death tolls given in the chronicles and in turn draw some conclusions about the numbers of men engaged in combat? Casualty figures of well over 30,000 are given by some sources, and one can accept that this figure may be accurate for losses on the field, drownings in the two rivers at Towton and Tadcaster and deaths from wounds in the aftermath. However, it is questionable whether more than 25 per cent of the total combatants were killed on the battlefield itself. The rout is another problem entirely if the dead were spread over an area 6 miles long by 3 miles 4 furlongs wide.

In the letter read by William Paston in Chapter One, Edward IV informed his mother, Cicely Neville, the Duchess of York, that 20,000 Lancastrians were killed at the battle of Towton, and, judging by the heralds' estimates, 8,000 Yorkists.[4] The Milanese merchant Pigello Portinaro also received news from London that 20,000 Lancastrians and 8,000 Yorkists were killed, which not only further corroborates the above, but also confirms approximate figures by Abbot Whethamstede, Polydore Vergil, 'The Rose of Rouen' and the bishops of Salisbury and Exeter. Thus a death toll of between 20,000 and 28,000 from one original contemporary source, possibly one of those discussed in Chapter One, seems to be a reasonable approximation, of which figure the Lancastrians had the greater loss of life. The rout at the battle of Towton undoubtedly claimed many lives as the bloodletting continued, but the problems of accounting for these lives with any accuracy are immense.

I am inclined to believe that around 10,000 men may have been killed on both sides on the battlefield of Towton itself, 5,000 more of the Lancastrians in the immediate rout across the plateau to the River Cock and even more ultimately in the general pursuit to Tadcaster where further drownings and killing occurred. More soldiers were obviously injured in battle and consequently, in the medieval era, died from infected wounds after the event. Even my approximations regarding casualties are horrifying to comprehend and need no further exaggeration, given that these figures refer to deaths before mechanized warfare.

As a matter of interest, since it is a common misunderstanding by some, Edward Hall's figure of 36,766 for the dead at Towton is not only based on deaths 'on the field'. Instead it represents the death tolls for both sides over a four-day period, taking into account the battle of Ferrybridge, the skirmish at Dintingdale and the protracted pursuit from the field, as well as the main engagement of Towton. It is quite obvious, even discarding the larger casualty figures of Hall and accepting the lower estimates of deaths on the field and in the rout of, say, between 20,000 and 28,000, that the battle of Towton is Britain's bloodiest pitched battle.

So much for calculations, which play a part in understanding the battle's large format. However, for a commander such as the Duke of Somerset or Edward IV it is more likely that their visual appreciation of the marshalling troops would have been far different, and they certainly would not have been counting the numbers of men with their fingers. An impression of strength would have been far more valuable to them and their chief captains, coupled with an understanding of which nobles were present on the opposing side, pinpointed by their heraldic banners and standards.

In my view it is a very dangerous and fruitless enterprise for anyone to try to quote estimated figures on medieval battlefields with any accuracy, and, in studying the battle of Towton, playing around with noughts only complicates the issue.

The Yorkist Advance

Whichever theory we accept concerning the approach march of both armies to the battlefield of Towton, at some point one army would occupy a better position than the other, either by chance or by design. If, according to Jean de Waurin, Edward marched the main Yorkist army towards Towton from perhaps Sherburn-in-Elmet on the morning of 29 March, at some stage his army would have had to ascend the plateau to meet the Lancastrians in battle, just the same as if they had spent the previous night around Saxton and Lead waiting for contingents to arrive from the direction of Ferrybridge. More important, however, as far as the positions of the two armies is concerned, is that, according to Edward Hall, both forces were out of sight of each other during the final movements onto the battlefield because, 'when each party perceived each other they made a great shout, and at the same instant time there fell snyt [sleet?] or snow'.[5]

The lie of the land holds the clue to this statement by Hall, who places the Yorkist advance in battle formation up from the vicinity of Saxton, totally concealed by the southern plateau's height, until they reached the crest of the ridge above the depression where shouts of defiance came from both armies once they were in sight of each other. These few lines by the Tudor chronicler also further disprove the theories of a Lancastrian battle position on this southern ridge overlooking Saxton and Dintingdale, because, if the Duke of Somerset had formed his army up here, it would have been in full view of the Yorkists, similar to Richard III's vaward at the battle of Bosworth, stretching forth 'a wondrous length'[6] on the crest of Ambion Hill. Equally the theories of a Lancastrian position on the southern ridge between the hawthorn tree and Castle Hill Wood are very doubtful, considering that part of the Lancastrian battle-line, namely its right flank, would have had its back to the steep slopes of Bloody Meadow and the River Cock valley, an unenviable tactical position for any army.

Before the armies moved into position, mass would have been given by the various priests in the army, the church playing a very important part in the preparation for battle for knights and commoners alike, especially on such an uncertain Palm Sunday morning. Neither army, however, seems to have been one bit concerned about fighting and possibly dying on such a holy day – quite the reverse in fact. Vengeance, bloodlust, orders of no quarter, the killing of traitors and the resignation to kill or be killed echoed in the ranks. Edward's orders of no quarter are typical under the circumstances and comparable to similar feelings of those who had already lost their fathers or sons in the wars on the Lancastrian side. For some the imminent battle was to be the zenith of a quest for revenge that had been exposed like an undressed wound ever since the first battle of St Albans in 1455, when executions of such nobles as Somerset and Northumberland had caused their sons to scowl on the house of York and half unsheath their unblooded swords in venomous contempt. So it was for young Edward not only in his own search for the killers of his father and brother at Wakefield, but also now he had the opportunity to cut a clear path to the throne for himself in the process as an extra incentive. In this frame of mind, Edward must have regretted King Henry's absence on the battlefield, because, unlike his father, the Duke of York, it is doubtful whether he would have given the anointed king such fair treatment under the same circumstances. Later in 1471 he had Henry murdered in the Tower of London after the battle of Tewkesbury. Who knows what would have happened to poor King Harry after the battle of Towton?

Depending on whether you were Yorkist or Lancastrian, there were traitors to get even with as well. Sir Andrew Trollope and Lord Grey of Ruthin, to name but two, had already changed sides in the conflict, and it would not be the end of this behaviour by a long chalk. In Trollope's case we can have some sympathy for his predicament in that, because of his loyalty to King Henry in 1459, he had not only become the perpetrator of the Yorkist defeat at Ludford Bridge, and thus an enemy to Edward's regime, but had also become a dangerous military brain in the service of the Lancastrians. As such, £100 had been placed on his head, and the heads of some other named men, in the battle to come.

Certainly by late morning (9 o'clock according to Edward Hall) the two massive armies were in sight of each other, and most probably it was the Lancastrians, considering their presence on the plateau first, who had the best opportunity to choose the ground and consolidate their position on it. Lord Clifford's sacrificial abandonment may have been the cost of concealing this prepared plan of action – prepared in so much as Sir Andrew Trollope and the Duke of Somerset may have had some plan formulated to trick the Yorkists, such as an ambush like that at the battle of Wakefield or a similar tactical ploy, was perhaps foreseen by the duke and his chief military adviser. It is unreasonable to suggest, given the Lancastrian track record since Trollope joined their ranks, that the Master Porter of Calais would not have deliberately swayed his overmighty and surly young benefactor into a very strong position on the battlefield plateau with his keen tactical eye.

It would have undoubtedly taken some time for the two armies to get into battle array between Towton and Saxton, and trumpets, drums and shouts from captains, muffled by the wind, would have formed the men. Although most soldiers who had horses would have dismounted by this time, especially the archers, the darting to and fro of horsemen to deliver messages, and round up stragglers and faint hearts, would still have been apparent. The large baggage parks behind both armies would have been bustling with activity earlier on, as horses were tethered, weapons supplied and what little food and drink the army had with it were distributed to the men, but now, as the armies faced each other, only the extinguished fires, smoking between the wagons, and the guards around the perimeter would have been visible.

Both Yorkist and Lancastrian commanders would have consulted yet again with God before the final moves were underway. It is recorded that, before the battle of Agincourt, Henry V heard mass three times and took communion, as did most of his followers. This observance was a very important part of a Christian king or chivalrous knight's routine before battle, especially when, in his eyes, the power of God was far greater than the power of man in such matters of uncertainty. Of greater and more down-to-earth tactical importance, however, were the orders from the commander-in-chief and his captains, as, even with God on their side, military science was well established in English armies and proven tactics walked hand-in-hand with religious observance.

English captains took their art very seriously indeed and they organized men into companies and contingents that formed the usual three 'wards' or 'battles' of the era. The two variations of the battle formation were, by the fifteenth century, in line abreast or in line astern, and split 'vaward' or vanguard to the right or in front (foreward) of the army, 'mainward' or middleguard in the centre and 'rearward' or rearguard to the left, or taking up position at the back of the column or extended line. Other variations did exist when space was not available, but this was generally the organization of medieval English armies, even on their approach march to encounter the enemy. At this point the vaward would arrive on the battlefield first to cover the advance of the two remaining wards, as Fauconberg's archers would have done the night before the battle, it being well supplied with bows and, more often than not, much enlarged to give battle first if needed. Even this tactic was not, however, cast in stone, and on several occasions in the Wars of the Roses, battles formed up opposite each other purely out of choice or mistake.

Of the three main arms of bows, bills and men at arms it is uncertain whether bows alternated with knots of men at arms and bills at Towton, similar to the formation adopted by the English at Agincourt, or bows in fact fronted the battles with the rest filling in behind. I am inclined to believe the latter because of the events surrounding the opening stages of the battle of Towton, and I further suggest that the Yorkist vaward was wholly comprised of longbowmen in separate contingents under their captains and massed together as a very effective missile formation with one overall commander. Probably ten thousand men strong, and given the lie of the land, compacted into a ten-man-deep chequerboard formation, this arrangement would have given each archer not only room to reload, but also the ability to view his target slightly better. The second of the army's battles astern, because of the plateau's width, would have comprised the heavy infantry of knights, men at arms, billmen and mercenary companies, who would inevitably have to sustain the brunt of the fighting when the longbow had done its deadly work. This Yorkist division was undoubtedly commanded by Edward and Warwick. The rearward would in Towton's case have been a reserve made up of all arms contingents, and would have contained some mounted troops to sweep the rear of the army, plugging gaps and, more important, dissuading deserters with their fifteen-foot lances. These lighthorsemen were called 'prickers' for several good reasons as their name suggests (killing deserters, killing and pursuing routed troops, securing food, scouting in enemy territory and so forth).

In discussing further the Yorkist advance onto the battlefield, and also the position of both armies' battles before the main assault, it is important that we first take a look at the possibility of a Yorkist arrival first on the plateau, because this theory could further disprove historians' claims that the armies' opening battle-lines were somewhere other than across the depression. If the Yorkists occupied the southern ridge first, between the Tadcaster–Ferrybridge road and Bloody Meadow, taking the hawthorn tree as a command position, then the Lancastrians would have had no alternative but to advance to conform as much as possible with their enemy's frontage. As was usual in the Wars of the Roses the vawards inevitably implemented this manoeuvre to begin the archery duel, which more often than not decided who would advance first. Polydore Vergil told of an interesting development in the Lancastrian camp on the morning of the battle of Towton:

> It came to pass by mean of the soldiers, who, as their manner is, like not upon lingering, that very self same day, by day break in the morning, after he [Henry VI] had with many words exhorted every man to do his duty, he was forced to sound the alarm. His adversaries were there as ready as he.[7]

We could deduce from this passage that the Lancastrians were caught unawares, especially if, as according to Jean de Waurin, Edward marched to the battlefield during the early morning of 29 March. But more than this, if the Lancastrians were slow to move their army in any case then, forgetting de Waurin's comments, this would account for the better position of the Yorkist army and the cramped conforming battle array of the Duke of Somerset's forces across the depression. Trying to deploy the massive army under his command on the Battle Cross Ridge must have been a headache for the young duke, especially with other unruly nobles to contend with.

In my opinion, however, Somerset's army was in position on the plateau first, as this was by far the main objective of the Lancastrian command all along, because, in occupying the Battle Cross Ridge, this left the Yorkists disadvantaged by a similar space problem, which may not be immediately apparent. The reasoning behind this is that, in conforming to the Lancastrian battle-line, the greater amount of space available to the Yorkists on the southern ridge would have been wasted. It would have been pointless for the Yorkists to spread their army any further towards Castle Hill Wood where their archers, overlooking the area of the River Cock, would have had nothing to shoot at. Therefore the Lancastrians, straddled between Renshaw Wood and the steep banks of the River Cock to their right, and the Ferrybridge road marshes to their left, occupied a very strong and sound defensive position. If their archers also planted sharpened wooden stakes before them, as was usual practice in medieval battles, the slope before them, possibly slightly steeper in 1461, would have presented

Edward IV with a difficult frontal assault, that is providing the Lancastrian longbowmen won the archery duel and made the Yorkists advance first.

The wait for both armies' contingents to come up during the advance may have been long, and much heavy drinking on both sides might have quelled fear and numbed senses, especially among the Yorkist soldiers, who would have become drunk very quickly on their empty stomachs. John Keegan in *The Face of Battle* has this to say about the battle of Agincourt:

> The English who were on short rations presumably had less to drink than the French, but there was drinking in the ranks on both sides during the period of waiting and it is quite possible that many soldiers in both armies went into the mêlée less than sober, if not indeed fighting drunk. . . . The prospect of battle, excepting the first battle of a war or a green unit's first blooding, seems always to alarm men's anxieties, however young and vigorous they be, rather than excite their anticipation. Hence the drinking which seems an inseparable part both of preparation for battle and of combat itself. Alcohol, as we know, depresses the self-protective reflexes, and so induces the appearance and feeling of courage.[8]

Much has been said and written about the heraldic pomp and almost tacky lavishness of a medieval spectacle such as would have been witnessed as the two armies assembled for the battle of Towton. However, the truth about the appearance of not only the common soldiers, but also the medieval knights on the field of battle must have been far removed from Arthurian legend. In the first place the shivering recruits waiting for action may still have been wrapped in additional clothing, such as cloaks, and their once-resplendent livery jackets, now ingrained with grime and mud from the march, must have made identification far from easy. Their weapons, however, would have been in good order – the inspections by captains would have made sure of this – and the trusty longbow would have been well looked after, being bagged when not in use and meticulously honed by its owner, like all of the best missile weapons, in readiness for the attack.

Armour, especially the noble's expensive suits, was looked after and cleaned by pages, but most of the Yorkist men at arms, at any rate, were probably encased in plate for some time in anticipation of battle, and in this event rusting around joints and rivets may have been apparent due to the bad weather. However, as the nobles rode along the ranks of these cheering bedraggled, bawdy and unkempt troops, it is they alone who must have represented a lavish vision of medieval splendour to their men, and that sight at least must have boosted morale, especially if the man looked up to was a potential King of England.

Tens of thousands of Englishmen and their allies in thick grey-steeled phalanxes, spiked with lethal blades of destruction and pent up bows of Spanish yew, now faced each other in grim resolve to await their orders. Beneath stiff banners treated with buckram, to set permanently 'on the fly', eagle eyes strained to see their enemies' first move through the driving snow. It was to be the Yorkists who would take the initiative, and with this first step probably cause the biggest exchange of longbow 'fire' in recorded history.

The Archery Duel

Everyone in Northern Europe after the Hundred Years War knew the potential of the English longbow, especially the French, who had fallen victim to its killing power on several occasions. Because of this power, by the Wars of the Roses, horses and men in particular became even better armoured with designer plates, shaped and curved to deflect the cloth yard arrow with its bodkin-shaped head. Many other types of head and weights of arrow were used for different purposes in battle, but the common longbow, with a 100–150 lb draw weight and an effective range of up to 300 yards, was devastating enough with these specifications, if shot quickly and by the right number of men, to wreak havoc in even the best-protected ranks of men purely by causing disarray. At long range this was exactly the result of prolonged shooting. At closer range the longbow was even more lethal, penetrating plate armour, if the trajectory of an arrow was approximately ninety degrees to the surface, and skewering anything else in its path, through flesh and bone up to the goose feathers at its end.

However, the real strength of the longbowman was his rate of fire, estimated at between ten and fifteen arrows a minute. Only by law-enforced practice at the butts from an early age was this achieved, and, as Bishop Latimer recorded, this was by his day a time-honoured tradition to which all the Towton archers owed their great skill:

In my time my father was diligent to teach me to shoot, as other fathers were with their children. He taught me how to draw, how to lay my body to the bow, not to draw with the arms as other nations do, but with the strength of the body. I had my bows brought to me, according to my age, and as I increased so my bows were made bigger, for men shall never shoot well unless they are brought up to it.[9]

The archery duel at the battle of Towton was particularly and uniquely one sided, unlike some other engagements in the Wars of the Roses, when the longbow's effective sting was invariably cancelled out because of each side's knowledge and use of the weapon. One of the chroniclers is more certain about this phase of the battle than any other. Edward Hall gave the details of who was in command of the Yorkist archers, what effect the weather had on both sides' volleys of arrows and what the Lancastrians suffered when the clattering mass of missiles reached their target:

The Lord Fauconberg, which led the forward of King Edward's battle being a man of great policy and of much experience in martial feats caused every archer under his standard to shoot one flight and then made them stand still. The northern men, feeling the shoot, but by reason of the snow, not perfectly viewing the distance between them and their enemies [the snow and wind was driving into the Lancastrian faces from the south] like hardy men shot their sheaf arrows as fast as they might, but all their shot was lost and their labour in vain for they came not near the southern men by 40 tailors yards. When their shot was almost spent the Lord Fauconberg marched forward with his archers, who not only shot their own sheaves, but also gathered the arrows of their enemies and let a great part of them fly against their own masters, and another part they let stand on the ground which sore annoyed the legs of the owners when battle was joined.[10]

Polydore Vergil confirmed the obvious fact that 'the archers began the battle, but when their arrows were spent the matter was dealt by hand strokes'.[11] Whatever transpired when the Yorkist archers advanced after their first flight of arrows and delivered more similar barrages at the Lancastrians, it was annoying enough to force the issue. In fact the arrow storm must have been so devastating in the ranks of the lesser armoured archers fronting the army that, at this range, possibly three hundred yards across Towton Dale and North Acres, the tendency must have been for some of the Lancastrians to fall back out of the way of the withering fire. In the chronicles of Jean Froissart some Genoese crossbowmen were at a similar disadvantage at the battle of Crécy when

> The English archers took one pace forward and poured out their arrows on them so thickly and evenly that they fell like snow. When they felt these arrows piercing their arms, their heads and their faces, the Genoese, who had never met such archers before, were thrown into confusion. Many cut their bowstrings and some threw down their crossbows and began to fall back.[12]

The bitterly cold driving snow and wind must have seemed insignificant to the Lancastrian bowmen, as wave after wave of hissing arrow shafts clattered and thudded into their ranks on the Battle Cross Ridge. Their adversaries' volleys would have impeded their own fire, and possibly pierced many so as to look like 'hedgehogs with quills', according to an earlier chronicler's observation of Scottish troops under similar circumstances. If the '40 tailors yards' (60 yards) shortfall of arrows is to be believed, then, at a range of approximately 300 yards, the wind must have been either very strong to slow the Lancastrian missiles, or the distance to the Yorkist lines was badly judged by Lancastrian captains due to poor visibility. Whatever the problem, things went very badly for the Lancastrians and the usual archery duel rapidly developed into a one-sided turkey shoot in favour of the Yorkists. The incessant orders of 'notch, stretch, loose' or 'knock, draw, loose' by the Yorkist vaward captains must have unleashed intermittent showers of arrow shafts by contingents, rather than a complete rhythmic one volley at a time burst towards the Lancastrian position because of the length of the battle-lines. In reply the Lancastrian volleys must have been a lot more erratic due to their increasing casualties and disarray. Lord Fauconberg had judged the following south-easterly wind well, but one must say that it was pure luck that it was there to carry the Yorkist arrows with ease to their target. However, considering that arrows climbed to a height of about a hundred feet in some instances, and had to achieve from this a very narrow zone of impact to have the desired effect, the skill, especially in the weather conditions at Towton, is awe-inspiring. The wind and driving snow was certainly disadvantageous for the Lancastrians as, contrary to their plans, and because of the withering fire and mounting casualties, they had no alternative but to begin to advance first and give up their defensive position on the ridge.

The Lancastrian Advance

Stepping over the bodies of their fallen comrades and possibly half a million fallen arrows, a large unwieldy mass of full and partially steel-clad men at arms and billmen began to move forward. Helmets and visors were adjusted into position, weapons were drawn or clutched in tighter grips and the nobles dismounted from their war horses to lead their retainers and household men into battle. This act of dismounting was 'the English manner'[13], as described by Philip de Commynes, and, apart from being a very good idea to vest positive morale into the contingents led by the nobles, it was also a risky business because, once battle was joined and the weapons started to fly, difficult situations in the mêlée could quickly develop into confusion, and the chance of being surrounded with no escape became an awful reality. Prominent nobles were more often than not killed in the Wars of the Roses by complying with this typically English fashion, which owes its place more to officers in wars of the nineteenth and twentieth centuries than to the medieval battlefield knight.

One of the other reasons for this levelling of the classes in battle was more practical than this, because, as the knight on horseback became more and more a target for the longbowman, and consequently at the mercy of serious injuries, which could be inflicted by falling and being trampled by his horse, or by others in similar circumstances, the English manner dictated that the knight's horse should only be used to carry him to the battlefield. Once there, he would immediately dismount and fight on foot. Senior commanders such as the Duke of Somerset and Edward IV may have kept their mounts for communication purposes at Towton, but even these men would also have dismounted for long periods of time and thrown themselves into the conflict when the need arose.

It is possible that the Earl of Northumberland, accompanied by Sir Andrew Trollope, led the first wave of dismounted heavy infantry across the valley to engage the enemy, sitting confidently on the opposite ridge, as this part of the Lancastrian battle-line may have been getting the worst of the barrage of arrows. Edward Hall depicts both men as commanding the Lancastrian vaward and, 'seeing their shot not prevail, hastened forward to join with their enemies'.[14] Jean de Waurin described Lord Rivers and the Duke of Somerset initiating a two-battle attack on the Yorkist line, with the Earl of Northumberland slowly moving forward on the other side of the field. With a blizzard of snow and arrows still mercilessly raining down on them, the Lancastrians, perhaps minus their archers, who may have fallen behind by this time, trudged on into the no-man's-land between the two armies.

The vaward followed suit behind the mainward in the attack and the Duke of Exeter's reserve brought up the rear, while the incessant loosing of arrows was kept up by the Yorkist archers until their supply was exhausted. Two sheaves of twenty-four arrows each would not have lasted very long, even with the retrieval of Lancastrian shafts from the fields in front of them and the possibility of replenishment by runners from the baggage train. However, many of the mainward, even well-armoured men at arms, would have been killed or wounded in the assault as the trusty longbow did its deadly work. Finding gaps in their continuously moving metal plates, especially at the joints, the steel-tipped arrows would have had no trouble in puncturing the chainmail and leather beyond. However, not all of the Lancastrians would have been so well armoured, because being mustered together as a contingent a structure of well-armoured gentry accompanied by their similarly armed retainers would have been leading others with only partial armour-plate, and jacks, brigandines and the like, covered by thin livery coats. These types of lesser armoured troops would have been fair game for the longbow's close quarter sting as the Lancastrian drums beat the advance.

When the Lancastrian army started to climb the Yorkist ridge, snipering by skirmishers would still have occurred, but a lull in the shooting may have been evident, and only at short range would the cracking and malfunctioning of some handguns, because of the foul weather, have been heard. Jean de Waurin gave a description of one of the Lancastrian attacking battles from the Yorkist viewpoint above Bloody Meadow and North Acres:

At that moment . . . [Edward IV] saw the army of the Earl of Northumberland coming for battle carrying the banner of King Henry. The Earl of March [Edward IV] rode his horse along his army where all the nobles were and told them how they had wanted to make him their king, and he reminded them that they were seeing the next heir to the throne which had been usurped by the Lancasters a long time ago. He suffered his troops and knights to help him now to recover his inheritance and they all assured him of their desire to help and said that if any wished not to fight they should go their own way. So all of them hearing this good request by the young earl, who was already thinking as a king, shouted in unison that they would follow him until death if necessary. Hearing this support the earl thanked them, jumped from his horse and told them, sword in hand, that on this day he would live or die with them in order to give them courage. Then he came in front of his banners and waited for the enemy which was marching forward with great noise and shouting 'King Henry!'[15]

Propaganda aside, the steady advance of cheering Lancastrians towards the Yorkist lines must have been a sight to snap anyone's nerves, and it was probably at this moment that the order was given for the Yorkist archers to fall back through the ranks so that heavier troops and men at arms could get to the front in time for the next phase of the battle.

This seemingly straightforward manoeuvre could not have been easy under the circumstances however, and it is foolish to think that lines of troops, especially a thousand yards in length, could have moved on the battlefield with Napoleonic precision, or all at once for that matter. Some confusion, indeed great panic, may have occurred when the order was given to retire, and in pushing through and round their own advancing mainward some longbowmen may have been irreverently jostled to the ground by their overconfident superiors. Other archers may have been caught up in the Lancastrian advance, as the chronicles suggest that Fauconberg's vaward was slightly stepped forward in front of the Yorkist main body. In any event this act of exchanging ranks must have occurred at some point during the Lancastrian attack, even if we accept the alternative three-battle formation abreast in a line, as a collision with practically defenceless longbowmen on this scale would have been catastrophic for the Yorkist army.

Apart from enduring the grim ordeal of their advance, and the mounting casualties incurred because of it, the Lancastrians, in moving to the attack at the same time, probably found more room to deploy their compacted army across the battlefield, especially on their right flank. Also, in so doing, it became increasingly obvious, as the Lancastrian mainward assaulted the southern ridge, that now the Yorkists must suffer what they must have been fearing all along – the weight of greater Lancastrian numbers against them. The real battle of Towton would be fought on the southern plateau, the most exposed tract of land in the area.

The Main Battle

Soon we shall see fields littered with quarters of helmets, and shields, and swords, and saddles, and men split through the trunk right to the belt . . . I tell you I have no such joy as when I hear the shout 'On, on!' from both sides and the neighing of riderless horses and groans of 'Help me, help me!' when I see both great and small fall into ditches and on the grass and see the dead transfixed by spear shafts! . . . When he's in the thick of it let no man of birth think of anything but the splitting of heads and arms, for a dead man is worth more than a live prisoner. . . . Barons, put in pawn castles and farms and towns, but never give up war![16]

Bertrand de Born graphically told of his own personal attitude towards the horror of battle, which probably comes very close to what most knights, and especially the nobles, must have believed and justified to others of similar status to themselves in the medieval period. The apocalyptic quest for destruction, the abandonment of others, merciless killing and the joy because of it, instinctive bloodlust to do more of the same, and the detachment and unconcern for the dead and dying are all apparent in the above passage, which reeks of bravado and unbounded selfishness by the perpetrator of such deeds, especially on the lower classes ranged like ninepins against him.

This state of mind by the aristocrats on both sides was most certainly apparent at the battle of Towton, and, as such, is a very important factor to bear in mind when trying to understand what a knight expected to do once hand-to-hand fighting began on the medieval battlefield. The lower classes, on the other hand, must have felt very different about the whole affair, and their concept of killing on this scale must have been a far more basic case of survival through all methods possible, which ultimately could include running away if the opportunity arose. As the Lancastrian army eventually came within fifty yards of the Yorkist battle-line, these recruits must have felt the same pangs of fright and gut-churning unease that any duty-bound soldier must endure. Most would have held all outward signs of this back in front of their comrades, shouting abuse at the enemy and taking part in their own forms of bravado in an attempt to cover up their apprehension about the inevitable clash of arms. Veterans would have known the desperate situation all too well, and also what to do and what to avoid in battle based on their past experiences of close-quarter fighting. However, for all men in the front line the rush of adrenaline was probably enough to sway the advancing ranks of steel against each other like a wave, pre-empting orders, and apparent enough to cause Edward and Warwick, commanding the Yorkist mainward, to initiate a charge at the Lancastrians to avoid disarray.

Slipping and sliding towards each other in a charge, more in slow motion than in keeping with a mounted attack, the two front ranks clashed upslope on the southern plateau of the battlefield. Filling out and finding more width as they advanced, the Lancastrians pushed into Bloody Meadow up the steep gradient, there incurring heavy casualties. All along the writhing front line, various forms of weapon would have been at work, beating down on their enemies' defences with deafening repetition, and attempting forward and backward movements in the limited space available. Some weapons may not even have been swung or caused any damage, because of the closely packed masses of men, and, in the push and shove from the rear, many stumbling unfortunates must have been caught under the metallic stampede, and simply crushed to death by friends and enemies without even landing a blow. Eyewitnesses to this type of death vouch for how commonplace a feature it was on the battlefields of the fifteenth century. Edward, Duke of York, at Agincourt was probably either killed by this kind of suffocation under falling masses of men or suffered a heart attack in much the same situation.

By midday the two remaining Lancastrian battles would have joined the fray, but in so doing would have caused more problems in their own front line. This effect of perpetually advancing ranks of men eager to be at the enemy, and the pushing and shoving from these rear ranks by those unaware of the situation at the front, would have contributed a great deal to casualties on both sides. The first heaps of dead recorded by the chroniclers may have been formed in this first assault, as Yorkists and Lancastrians stumbled back and forth on the snow-covered and arrow-strewn slopes of the depression, causing domino effects in the rear ranks of their unscathed and oblivious troops. As the third stage of the battle progressed, 'so great was the slaughter', according to Polydore Vergil, 'that the very dead carcasses hindered them that fought',[17] and because of this, gaps and areas of 'dead ground' would have appeared between the two armies, clogged with barriers of corpses and fallen weapons.

In such an event the tendency would have been for troops either to clamber over the top of such an unsteady platform to encounter the enemy, or to go around the obstacle in the hope of finding a better foothold somewhere else. Thus pockets of fighting would have occurred all along the battle-line, making shoring up the front ranks a continuous headache for the captains because, once exploited, these gaps could immediately be turned to advantage if the ground was won or left unguarded. Nobles, accompanied by their retainers, would have disputed these narrow defiles on foot, in large fighting groups under their battle banner and working as a team. In the bloody hand-to-hand fighting that would have followed, the aim was for the retainers to cut a swathe through the enemy and forge a route for the noble to advance his banner, thus a rallying point was established and the rest of the battle followed, gradually making ground in the process. Movements such as this, however, must have been far from straightforward or technical under battle conditions and, apart from battle banner or standard recognition, all troops must have looked very similar as the battle wore on. As the orders in the chain of command became more and more garbled, some troops must have been confused as to whether they were landing blows on the enemy or, accidentally, on their friends.

In payment for livery jackets the Nottingham chamberlain's accounts recorded that 'red cloth' was purchased 'for soldiers jackets and white fustian to make letters, and for the cutting out and threading on the letters'.[18] However, red jackets were a common uniform colour in the Wars of the Roses, and as for the recognition letters of their company, who would be looking in the heat of the battle? The only way to minimize mistakes in such a mêlée was to fight in close order as a group, thus the 'team' was managed better as a fighting unit, and morale was instilled more efficiently either by words or personal feats in arms by the captains. If this formation was achieved in such an attack, unit defensive formations could be adopted and rallying points established for rest and reorganization. Polydore Vergil, in describing the battle of Bosworth, had this to say about the martial attributes of Henry Tudor's chief vaward commander during the battle below Ambion Hill:

> In the mean time the Earl of Oxford, fearing lest his men in fighting might be environed of the multitude, commanded in every rank that no soldiers should go above 10 feet from the standards; which charge being known, when all men had throng thick together, and stayed a while from fighting, their adversaries were afraid, supposing some fraud, and so they all forbore the fight a certain space and that verily did many with right goodwill, who rather coveted the king [Richard III] dead than alive, and therefore fought faintly. Then the Earl of Oxford in one part, and others in another part, with bands of men close one to another, gave fresh charge upon the enemy, and in array triangle [a wedge formation] vehemently renewed the conflict.[19]

It is apparent from this account that the Earl of Oxford, in seeing a difficult situation developing, simultaneously rallied his men, confused his Yorkist enemies and reorganized his contingents into a strong battle formation, which was later to crush King Richard's vaward under the Duke of Norfolk. Actions such as this by commanders would have been commonplace in the Wars of the Roses, and of major importance when the recognition of troops was difficult or, as at Towton, when numbers were exceptionally large and confused. The mistaken identity of Oxford's troops returning to the field in thick fog, only to be shot at by their own men at the battle of Barnet, illustrates what could happen if the army's battles lost contact and the threatening aspects of treachery came into play.

As time passed between Towton and Saxton, and the bleak morning turned into an even bleaker afternoon with a leaden sky yielding yet more sleet and snow on the forces of York and Lancaster, both front lines continued with their grim task like thousands of foundry workers displacing and puncturing riveted metal plates and their contents within. One way in which a weapon such as the poleaxe or battle mace could crush an opponent's limbs or skull was by its owner repeatedly pounding away at one part of the metal defences until the resulting depression caused injury or alternatively rendered that part of the armour useless. When this was achieved, guards would inevitably come down as joints seized and the partially defenceless knight would be despatched, probably by others as well, through vulnerable gaps in the armour such as the armpit, the groin and the visor, with weapons specifically designed for that purpose.

As the battle became a one-to-one mêlée, a lightly armoured soldier like the longbowman also came into his own, using sword, buckler and small side-arms such as daggers, axes and mauls to defend himself. By carrying less weight and working in groups with these weapons, these nimble and bowless archers could quite easily catch men at arms and knights encased in armour at a disadvantage, singling them out to be killed if they were unsupported. The billman, carrying his trusty polearm, and others with similar shafted weapons such as the glaive, may have found that space was cramped in the early stages of the battle. The billman, like those who used the pike, which was not common in Britain at this time, needed enough room to wield his polearm to good effect, but as more space eventually opened up the bill became more effective, being particularly useful for both hooking an opponent to the ground, and then thrusting and chopping at him, thereby utilizing all three classic attacking movements in one weapon.

Distress and fatigue inevitably set in in some men and in whole contingents, and as this phase of the battle wore on the tendency would have been either simply to break off and try to retire or to be killed by a fresher or more experienced enemy. Because the commanders' orders of no quarter were quite specific at the battle of Towton and the ferocity more intense than usual, as this cry of alarm went up in the line it was the commander's job to plug the gap with fresh reserves or, in some instances, himself. Philip de Commynes stated that Edward IV won nine battles, 'all of which were fought on foot',[20] so there is no reason to doubt that he for one dismounted at crucial stages of the battle of Towton, his greatest triumph, to lead men into the thick of the fighting. Quite naturally we would expect no less from all of the battle commanders of both sides, including the Earl of Warwick, who may have been in great danger, possibly limping about the field because of the arrow wound sustained at Ferrybridge the previous day.

It may have been at this point in the battle, as the Lancastrians brought their greater numbers to bear, that the Yorkists were slowly pushed back, step by step, across their own opening battle-line onto the southern plateau. Gradually both armies moved towards Saxton, leaving behind them thousands of dead and wounded on the slopes of the depression, especially in Bloody Meadow and on the Lancastrian Battle Cross Ridge, where their vaward had fallen foul of the opening arrow fight with Lord Fauconberg. Was this sudden Lancastrian push just the effect of numbers overlapping the Yorkist left flank as more room was found to manoeuvre, or was there some more serious cause for the backtracking? After all, surely the extra Lancastrian manpower could not have been so telling at this time, as the inequality of numbers had presumably been redressed by the heavy casualties caused before and during the Lancastrian attack?

It is quite possible that, in addition to the effects of the overlapping mentioned above, a far more serious problem may have occurred on the Yorkist exposed left flank to cause not a parallel movement by Edward's hard-pressed army, but the development of a gradual pivoting angle in the Yorkist battle-lines, caused by a Lancastrian ambush emanating from Castle Hill Wood.

The Lancastrian Ambush

Apart from the various concepts of recent nineteenth- and twentieth-century historians, there is no contemporary evidence of an ambush or flank attack by the Lancastrians emerging from, or having its origin in, Castle Hill Wood, but still the story has been perpetuated. This sound, tactical prearranged secret weapon of the Lancastrian command has often been hinted at, but has never been supported by a scrap of evidence, apart from the musings of military probability. Analysing the ambush party theory without any such evidence, it is easy to discard the event as pure fantasy, or to accept the tactical possibility of such a manoeuvre without a thought as to its probability. I will try to shed more light on it in view of the facts that, first, an archaeological site may back up a significant weakening in Edward's army, second, the chronicles may indicate a serious Yorkist setback and, third, evidence of the ambush's devastating effect on the Yorkist battle-line may have manifested itself later on in the wars, to which Edward acted promptly to remedy a very similar threatening situation.

To address the problem fully, it is necessary to build a scenario in which we accept that the Lancastrians were in position first on the Battle Cross Ridge, and that an order for a mounted detachment of 'spears' to occupy Castle Hill Wood had been made before the Yorkists arrived on the field. This detachment was most probably located on the fringes of the wood, because even today this area is very densely covered with trees and undergrowth. Consequently, when the battle of Towton was fought it must have been an even more impassable feature and therefore totally unsuitable for cavalry other than on its outskirts. If a prearranged order was given for the spears to attack when the enemy was fully committed, the Lancastrian detachment may have chosen to charge the Yorkists no later than when their own army was beginning to push the enemy back up onto the southern plateau. Surprise would have been the key factor for the plan's success, and this would have been helped considerably by the effects of the falling snow, causing poor visibility for the Yorkists.

Once hit by such a shock tactic, part of the Yorkist line would almost certainly have buckled under the pressure and, now attacked on two fronts, inevitably fallen back, taking the remaining immediate lines with it. In a smaller army this assault by mounted men on unprepared, dismounted and fatigued infantry would have been enough to swing the battle in favour of the Lancastrians, and perhaps sufficient to cause panic and a Yorkist defeat. However, because of the unusually large numbers of men on the field and the distance of other troops from the problem, the Yorkists seem to have grimly held on.

As stated earlier, Richard Beauchamp, Bishop of Salisbury, received information that 'the result of the battle remained doubtful the whole of the day' and, 'at a moment when those present affirm that almost all of our followers despaired of it, so great was the power and impetus of the enemy'[21] that Edward, according to the bishop, stepped into the breach to stop the rot.

So significant was the despair because of the flank attack that, in my opinion, this caused both contending battle-lines to change alignment, and the Yorkist left flank, engaged by the ambush party, was at this point pushed down the south-west slope of the battlefield plateau, leaving the right flank still in the grip of bitter fighting in North Acres and above the depression. If this scenario is correct, the existence of the three burial mounds below Castle Hill Wood may corroborate that this major upset took place, resulting in some Yorkist casualties in the vicinity as they were cut down by the Lancastrian cavalry, while fleeing towards Lead and the banks of the River Cock. Further support for the ambush party theory is available if we take into account the comments of Jean de Waurin in his chronicle regarding the opening stages of the battle of Towton. We can also pin down the basic concept of a Yorkist disaster and apparent cause for concern in the army when some of Edward's troops routed unexpectedly on a wing and were chased from the battlefield. Edward, behind his banners at this time, saw the débâcle, and the seriousness of the catastrophe is underlined by his anger after the event:

> when Lord Rivers, his son [Anthony Woodville] and six or seven thousand Welshmen led by Andrew Trollope, following the Duke of Somerset himself with seven thousand men, charged his cavalry who fled and were chased for about eleven miles. It seemed that Lord Rivers' troops had won a great battle, because they thought that the Earl of Northumberland had charged on the other side, unfortunately he had not done so and this became his tragic hour for he died that day. During this débâcle many of the Earl of March's soldiers died and when he learned the truth of what had happened to his cavalry he was very sad as well as very annoyed.[22] [It is to be noted that during this period 'cavalry' or 'spears' were a general term for the infantryman or man at arms either mounted or dismounted.]

Apart from the ambush being a sound tactical plan to use an available terrain feature to achieve surprise, and two similar accounts to support possible archaeological evidence, there is tantalizing proof ten years later of Edward's fear of a similar ambush ploy at Tewkesbury by the Lancastrians. However, this time, with hindsight, he took immediate action even before the battle began. *The History of the Arrivall of Edward IV in England* provides the details:

> Here it is to be remembered that when the king [Edward IV] had come to the field, before he attacked, he considered that upon the right hand of the field was a park, with many trees. He, thinking to provide a remedy in case his said enemies had laid any ambush of horsemen in that wood, he chose out of his troops 200 spears and set them in a group together about a quarter of a mile from the battlefield, charging them to keep a close watch on that part of the wood, and do what was necessary if need should arise, and if they saw no such need to employ themselves in the best way they could.[23]

However eagle eyed King Edward's generalship may have been in spotting the potential danger of a surprise attack from the woods, we cannot get away from the fact that this type of ambush tactic was well known and highly likely as a ploy by the Lancastrians by the time of the battle of Tewkesbury in 1471. Could Edward's reconnaissance of the wooded park have been sparked by the memory of a similar situation, which caused a great deal of trouble at the battle of Towton?

It is very easy for us to sit in judgement on Edward's precautionary move at Tewkesbury, knowing all too well the folly of exposing one's flank to an unreconnoitred feature of the terrain – after all, the manoeuvre is a basic tactical safety measure. However, considering that open battle was generally more simplistic in the medieval period, we can only highlight that a successful ambush was far more serious then than it appears today. In fact it had already been so disastrous in the Wars of the Roses that it had swept away a rash move without proper precautions by Edward's father, the Duke of York, at the battle of Wakefield in 1460. I believe this is what the Duke of Somerset and Sir Andrew Trollope intended to do at the battle of Towton as the Yorkists exposed their flank to Castle Hill Wood, hence the Lancastrian army's initial position on the Battle Cross Ridge rather than on the southern plateau, where the woods and the ambush could not possibly have worked to such good effect.

The main plan would have been to draw the Yorkists on across the depression for what would then have been, in effect, a surprise attack by the ambush party at the rear of the Yorkist battle-line. This would have been a crippling prospect for the Yorkists, to say the least. Unfortunately, because of the abandonment of their position, the Lancastrian detachment had to settle for the Yorkist flank, which admittedly caused disarray and localized panic, but posed no irreversible problems for Edward's commanders in view of the numbers of men and ranks involved in defending the swing in the Yorkist front line.

Another major event at the battle of Towton may also point to why the Yorkists were able to hold on and temporarily retrieve the developing situation on their flank. This was because of another weakness, but this time in the Lancastrian army, and mentioned by Jean de Waurin in his chronicle. It seems that, as the Lancastrian army advanced, the Earl of Northumberland's battle was slow to engage the enemy and, because of this, was pushed back into North Acres by the Yorkists counterbalancing the effects of the ambush on their own flank. If this actually occurred, the Yorkists may have made some ground and thus, in the process, the battle-lines may have swung even farther, extending diagonally from North Acres to the very edge of the southern plateau, south-west of Castle Hill Wood. It was probably at this time, as the Lancastrian left was pushed back, that, according to Waurin, the Earl of Northumberland was struck down and, being severely wounded, was dragged to the rear.

The Yorkists give Ground

At least three chroniclers agree on the persistent snow storm during the battle of Towton. Hearne's Fragment maintains that 'all the while it snew',[24] and the Croyland chronicler has it that 'the snow covered the whole surface of the Earth'[25] after the battle. Edward Hall verifies the wintry conditions during the opening manoeuvres on the field and also in the archery duel, so in view of this, coupled with the long duration of the battle, we can imagine that conditions on Palmsunday Field were very poor by the afternoon. Even if the showers were intermittent, after three to four hours' fighting there must still have been a layer of snow partly covering piles of dead bodies and debris littering the battlefield, slowly concealing them altogether as more flakes fell. However, stained red with the blood of the dead, the dying and the fighting wounded, the ground must have been far from pretty. In fact the snow covering the battlefield would have changed colour due to churned up blood on the surface, and gradually turned to slush with the effect of thousands of men continually toing and froing over half-buried corpses. Because of this the results of smashed and butchered human remains would have been more apparent than usual in the telltale marks on the battle's white carpet, but even this did not cause a slackening in the soldiers' resolve to kill, and the slaughter continued amid the incessant cries of anguish and pain of battle.

The armoured knight in his sallet helmet, straining through eyeslots with blinkered vision and perspiring from the heat and pain caused by, among other things, chafing neck armour, cannot have lasted long in these conditions without rest. If he did not rest he was fair game not only to exhaustion, but also to dehydration, both of which could lead to death in the mêlée as reflexes became slower and blows from the helmeted head's blind side rendered the victim partially stunned, if not unconscious. Once down, fatal injuries would have been inflicted by the enemy, so it is obvious that such men at Towton did not fight for a full day under these conditions (ten hours, according to some chroniclers) or without some form of break.

Soldiers and full contingents had to come out of the front line for rest at some stage, under very difficult and confused circumstances, or instead be killed by the enemy and then irreverently stepped over by their comrades. When rest was possible, however – and the nobles were especially proficient at doing this because of their protective fighting units' cover – the first requirement was liquid. Off would come the helmet, and possibly the bevor (armoured neck protection), and immediately the unprotected knight was vulnerable, especially to missile fire. Lord Dacre of Gilsland may have done just this at the battle of Towton, and while drinking a cup of wine was hit in the neck or head by an arrow and fell dead in North Acres. The legendary 'lad' in a bur, or elderberry tree, who shot at him could have been almost anywhere on the battlefield, if indeed he existed at all. Tabards bearing the heraldic achievements of a lord or noble were not always worn in battle over armour in the Wars of the Roses, therefore the lone archer's recognition of Dacre, especially in the confusion of battle, is open to question, and a stray or ricocheting arrow is a more likely explanation for Dacre's death.

The lord's demise would certainly have affected his troops' morale, but how this manifested itself is hard to comprehend. Some of Dacre's men may understandably have looked over their shoulders if they were not fighting or otherwise occupied, but for many the bond of retainer may have compelled them to fight on because their name, as well as that of their overlord, would have been part of the attainder document issued by the winning side if they were to lose the battle and live. The laws of attainder required of whoever was marked down complete submission of land and titles in addition to the penalty of death for treason. So this threat more than any other may have been the compulsion that in the end made many men fight on, as either dead or alive they were subject to the 'bad blood' punishments of the victorious side's attainder. However, the local militiamen or levies, in such a soul-searching situation, were kept closely in check by their captain as it was they who could disappear into the background with ease after a battle and reappear without such an obligatory weight to bare on their shoulders. As such, these poor wretches were invariably made the fifteenth-century 'cannon fodder' of the battles, and it is certain that more of these common soldiers are buried on Palmsunday Field than any of their overlords or paymasters.

As the early afternoon of Palm Sunday approached, the human conveyor-belt of troops arriving in the front line must have included the reserves of the Duke of Exeter's Lancastrians and his counterparts on the Yorkist side, Wenlock and Dinham. It was at this time, as dismay crept into Yorkist hearts, that it seemed that the Lancastrian power would carry the day. Edward and his commanders, Warwick and Fauconberg, must have wondered if the Duke of Norfolk would ever arrive on the field, and also asked themselves not only would he be true to his word, but, if Norfolk did turn up, would it be only in time to see a severe Yorkist defeat. Edward's messengers must have reported back Mowbray's position at regular intervals throughout the day, but now, according to the chronicles, desperation was the order of the day and time was rapidly running out for the Rose of Rouen.

The Yorkist army was by this time still being pushed back in a great bulging mass, closer and closer to the downslope of Saxton, Dintingdale and Lead. Once reached, the terrain would undoubtedly have done its worst and taken its effect on the struggling and battle-worn troops, signalling disaster for the Yorkists after an unbelievable five hours of fighting.

In all of the chronicles recording King Edward IV's achievements, the stirring propaganda of his fighting ability comes flooding vividly across the centuries, similar in some respects to Henry V at his most glorious hour. Yet less is spoken, or indeed publicized, about the Yorkist warrior, who was more at home in battle than anywhere else. Later in his reign, Edward became a philanderer and womanizer, fat and tortured by his inactivity, and like an athlete who has outgrown his usefulness on the running track he sought other habits to fulfil his passion. However, at the battle of Towton he was a young man and by all accounts a giant of athletic proportions, so most chronicles affirm that it was his attributes alone as a killing machine that spurred his men on at this most desperate time. George Neville recorded in his letter to Coppini:

I prefer you should learn from others than myself how manfully our King, the Duke of Norfolk, and my brother and uncle bore themselves in this battle, first fighting like common soldiers, then commanding, encouraging and rallying their squadrons like the greatest captains.[26]

Pushing into the weakest part of the battle-line on foot with the Black Bull of Clarence carried by his standard bearer, Ralph Vestynden, Edward, with his household men, would have endeavoured to stabilize the ever-thinning line with reserves and rested troops. The twelve-foot-long battle flag of his ancestors would have served as a marker for all to see, and the line to rally behind and thus the breach would have been temporarily closed and morale boosted by the king's intervention on such a basic level. This passage in the *Arrivall* concerning the battle of Barnet vividly describes Edward and his fighting unit in action, and illustrates King Edward's strengths of courage and character at the maximum point of danger:

> with the faithful, well-beloved and mighty assistance of his fellowship, that in great number dissevered not from his person, and were well assured unto him as to them was possible, he manly, vigorously and valiantly assailed them, in the midst and strongest of their battle. Where with great violence, he beat and bare down afore him all that stood in his way and then turned to the range, first on one hand, and then on the other hand, in length, and so beat and bare them down, so that nothing might stand in the sight of him and the well assured fellowship that attended truly upon him.[27]

Stirring Yorkist propaganda this might be, but the facts concerning King Edward's exposure to danger must be appreciated in that those who knew him maintained that, by fighting on foot in all his battles, he not only encouraged others to greater personal prowess, but also caused a greater 'oneness' and unity in his army that went a long way to winning him his battles. In this battle-hardened frame of mind and with his strength of character, rather than his later stagnation, King Edward, in my opinion, was far better equipped both mentally and physically as a commander of men than any fighting monarch of England, including Henry V. At the battle of Towton, however, the future king's army may have been almost beaten by the early afternoon, and, for all his strength of character, things were going very badly indeed for the Yorkists. The Lancastrians' priority, sensing this advantage, must have been an even firmer determination to get at the usurper and quickly end the ordeal by flinging all that was left of their nobles and reserve contingents into the groaning mass of bodies for the final push. It is more than likely that, in this last ditch attempt to end the battle quickly, all of the nobles on both sides fought on foot. Judging by the forward push from their baggage park, the Lancastrians in particular were by now quite some way from their tethered horses. Because of this situation the Lancastrian nobles were in great danger as, like the Yorkists, each of their dwindling contingent's strength was eroded into confusion.

Norfolk's Flank Attack

Why, with such an apparent advantage in the closing stages of the fight on the plateau, did the Lancastrian battle-line suddenly crack after winning so much ground and causing so much uncertainty, damage and despair in the Yorkist army?

This singular episode in the last phase of the battle of Towton has been wholly attributed to the sudden effects of the Duke of Norfolk's 'battle' finally entering the strung-out mêlée and threatening the left flank of the Lancastrian army. However, as we shall see, the battle did not end quickly even after this, although the Lancastrians lost a significant number of men in the initial panic. Edward Hall, who gave the fullest account of Towton, was unsure why the Yorkists turned the tide at all, and, like most of his fellow battle chroniclers, attributed the Lancastrian rout to the outcome of Edward IV's great skill as a commander rather than a reinforcement or sudden flank attack by the Duke of Norfolk. Only the author in Hearne's Fragment mentions Norfolk by name and records that 'about noon the aforesaid, Duke of Norfolk, with a fresh band of good men of war came to the aid of the newly elected King Edward',[28] and that was the chronicler who told of the dubious night battle of Towton alluded to earlier. However, to substantiate this fact further, a similar Yorkist reinforcement is suggested in Polydore Vergil's history, written some fifty years after the battle. He stated that:

Thus did the fight continue more than 10 hours in equal balance, when at last King Henry [in this case probably the Duke of Somerset] espied the forces of his foes increase, and his own somewhat yield, whom when by new exhortation he had compelled to press on more earnestly, he with a few horsemen removing a little out of that place, expected the event of the fight, but behold, suddenly his soldiers gave the back, which when he saw this he fled also.[29]

To this reinforcement we must also add the telling effects of the unusually long duration of the battle, and in the confusion it must have been apparent as the fighting continued that the scales had become so delicately balanced that either side, given even a slight advantage, could claim victory at any moment. Clearly the Yorkists would not have held on much longer if something very important and immediately telling had not occurred to turn the tide and indeed bolster the retreating ranks of their hard-pressed army. Already such men as Robert Horne, Lord Scrope and Sir Richard Jenney had been struck down and dragged out of the mêlée to the rear by their loyal retainers, suffering from severe wounds. The Kentish captain and Sir Richard were eventually to die on the field, but even this may not have been enough to make their contingents panic, provided the rest of the line did not crumble because of another commander's death. As for the effects on the common soldiers' demise in battle, there could be little or no help and, in terms of affecting morale, this cannot have been an issue if, once again, the line remained solid. As the Lancastrians continued their push, these incapacitated victims of their own army's retreat were now quite literally behind enemy lines and as such were soon finished off by the enemy bringing up the rear, killing and looting as they went.

Taking the Yorkist reinforcement in the afternoon of 29 March as being possible then, can we make any assumptions about where it was used to such good effect and what then happened to the Lancastrians because of it? From the point of view of the Duke of Norfolk's troops, as they approached the battlefield up the Ferrybridge road, the whole affair must have looked very confusing as the southern rim of the plateau came into sight. The main Yorkist army must at this time still have been holding the Lancastrian line from North Acres to the south-west edge of the plateau because, pushed any farther back, they would have encountered the downslope and cracked immediately. Therefore, apart from isolated details of movement on the ridge itself, the duke (or possibly his chief captain) may have chosen to continue, now admittedly with some urgency, farther up the road, sending out couriers to make contact with his king. It is very doubtful that Norfolk (if he was present in person) could have seen the hard-pressed left flank of the Yorkist army struggling badly on the other side of the battlefield, or been able to make out a battle at all from the Ferrybridge road position, or even from the high ground of Windmill Hill, to his left.

It is more than likely that, because of this confusion and urgency, Mowbray's forced-marched contingents 'found' their Yorkist allies as they manoeuvred around the right of the southern plateau into the depression.

Here they probably picked their way up the snow-covered slopes and quickly engaged the enemy with their stunned but grateful comrades, oblivious to what was going on.

If a judgement has to be made on what happened to the Lancastrian army at the battle of Towton, I suggest that it began in North Acres where the Yorkist right flank was probably the strongest. As the White Lion standard of the Duke of Norfolk was seen by the Lancastrian pressurized flank, the sight of fresh troops arriving on the scene must have immediately panicked their already battle-fatigued ranks and threw their formation into confusion. Worse still, the Yorkist battle-line on this flank was soon considerably extended as more and more men overlapped the enemy front, and suddenly a mighty cheer rose as a trickle of Lancastrian fugitives sped to the rear in panic.

With the fainthearted in flight it was now up to the battle-hardened veterans to stave off defeat on that side of the field. However, this was not now possible, due to the overwhelming Yorkist numbers and the effects of an already long, hard battle. One man after another looked to his neighbour for support as backs turned, only to be struck down from behind, making retreat inevitable for the whole contingent. This was probably the worst position any man of courage could find himself in because, while supported and facing front with his company's weapons bristling, he was still a formidable obstacle to be overcome by the enemy, but in hand-to-hand combat the greatest physical as well as psychological asset to the enemy was for the opposition to turn their backs in retreat. Certainly more casualties were inflicted by this attempt to break off from the enemy than any other single event in medieval battle. This problem was just as apparent at Towton as the first cracks in the Lancastrian battle-line rang the death knell of defeat all along the war-weary mass of men.

The tremor in the Duke of Somerset's army must have been almost like a rolling wave, as more and more contingents suffered from this similar increasing pressure on their left flank. At last the strongest part of the army, which had pushed the Yorkists back initially, turned in horror to witness their own men retreating in disorder across the body-strewn battlefield. In short, the Yorkists had hit the Lancastrians at their weakest point and consequently the battle-lines swung even more diagonally across the plateau, now almost at right angles to the armies' opening positions across the depression.

Even at the Lancastrian strong point on their right flank, some men now would have panicked and struggled to get away, while others, because of this, were cut down by the Yorkists. As a result the compacted ranks suddenly opened up and great yawning gaps appeared as knots of men attempted to flee, but were temporarily pushed back in by their leaders' poleaxes. Here standards wavered, and under them some nobles and their loyal retainers may have fought on against the odds, as bits of their front line disappeared to the rear and packs of preying Yorkists encircled to cut off their retreat. Once outnumbered the nobles would have been targeted and bludgeoned to the ground, and, because of this, difficulties may have arisen for the Yorkist captains in stopping the inevitable plundering of bodies that would have been commonplace on the field.

Because of this plundering the Yorkists may not have pursued the enemy immediately, as many of the Lancastrian nobles' rings, purses, weapons and armour were cut from their still dying bodies by more than eager Yorkist soldiers. Certainly the motivation and indeed the strength after such a long struggle must have been sadly lacking anyway for an immediate pursuit on foot, and because of this, coupled with the disorganization of the Yorkists, the Lancastrians may have been able to rally and form pockets of resistance along their ever-thinning line. Breathing heavily into the cold air and unbuckling their helmets for one last attempt to stop a complete massacre, armour may have been discarded as the brief pause in the fighting warned them of the possible consequences of running in full armour-plate.

As the clusters of Lancastrian resistance braced themselves for a further enemy charge, some of the more alert among them may have seen hundreds of mounted men with spears filling the gaps in the Yorkist line where they expected to see infantry emerge. Hearts sank as from beneath the tattered remnants of the once-resplendent Lancastrian standards came the piercing shriek to run.

The Rout and Pursuit

Philip de Commynes wrote in his memoirs after visiting the English court:

> King Edward told me that in all the battles which he had won, as soon as he had gained victory, he mounted his horse and shouted to his men that they must spare the common soldiers and kill the lords, of which none or few escaped.[30]

Thus it was at the battle of Towton when the Lancastrians eventually broke, and when, more out of practical necessity than tradition, the Yorkist horses were brought forward from the baggage park to be mounted for the expected pursuit. The Croyland chronicler took up the story in his usual Armaggedon style:

For their ranks being now broken and scattered in flight, the king's army eagerly pursued them, and cutting down the fugitives with their swords, just like so many sheep for the slaughter, made immense havoc among them for a distance of 10 miles as far as the city of York. Prince Edward, however, with part of his men as conqueror, remained upon the field of battle, and awaited the rest of his army, which had gone in various directions in pursuit of the enemy.[31]

The previous orders of no quarter mentioned by Edward Hall in his chronicle now probably became a free for all, as the Yorkist cavalry sprang from their exhausted ranks of foot after the stumbling and fleeing Lancastrians. However, clearly with the rout underway the main targets were the nobles in this bloody pursuit, especially those with price tags such as Sir Andrew Trollope, and those hunted by blood feud or land-hungry enemies. With such a great opportunity as this in his grasp at last, King Edward must have been determined to fulfil his own ambitions to the limit, and ensure that every effort was made to sweep what was left of Lancastrian resistance away from his throne. To this end all of the Yorkists were ordered to aim for the nobility, not only for the spoils of war, admittedly one of the reasons men took up arms in the first place, but also for the rewards that could be gained from killing their domestic and local enemies with their sovereign's consent.

The obvious place for the Lancastrian army to run was back in the direction from which they had marched a few days earlier, but this involved first crossing the River Cock, then the larger River Wharfe at Tadcaster. Also, now that the battle-lines had been altered, their route was being further dictated by their Yorkist pursuers towards the precipitous sloping edge of the plateau, which became the Lancastrian fugitives' first obstacle to overcome in their bid to stay alive.

It is almost impossible to descend any of the western edge of Towton battlefield without breaking into a run, and it is even more dangerous in wet or snowy weather to keep a sure footing, or indeed defy the effects of gravity, as the River Cock pulls you to its banks. It goes without saying then that this also happened to the Duke of Somerset's panic-stricken and broken army when, running at breakneck speed, they encountered the snow-covered edges of the plateau then the river beyond. Some armoured gentry may never have recovered from the hundred foot drop as they were irreverently pushed over the precipice by Yorkist 'spears', their heavy spinning bodies taking others with them on their journey to the bottom. Some Lancastrians may have sought refuge in Renshaw Wood, and made good their escape under its cover to the fords over the river, only to find their route cut off by Yorkists who were already making short work of many of their comrades trying to cross there.

By far the worst place encountered by the Lancastrian routing army must have been the 'funnel' of Towton Dale, and, for a second time in only a few hours, Bloody Meadow. Here, where the plateau's descent is not as steep, the Yorkist horsemen must have had a field day and inflicted a vast amount of casualties. Because of the dale's easy access, the crowding here must have been terrible, and, unlike most of the steeper slopes of the western edge of the battlefield, this area was more suitable for cavalry action right to the banks of the river. In fact this is probably how the Yorkist pursuers entered the valley of the River Cock in the first place, to strike all along its course at the struggling Lancastrians trying to cross its icy waters. It is highly unlikely that the Yorkists would have attempted to drive their horses down any of the other steep snow-covered slopes of the plateau, so instead they probably fanned out along its edge, running through the Lancastrians with their lances as they went. Finally, the vast majority of these confused fugitives were herded towards the easy access points to the River Cock, their only line of retreat, and were in the end attempting to cross there in their thousands.

Here the legendary bridges of bodies were built up as, one after another, the Lancastrian troops tried to wade across the deep gully that formed the river bed, only to be slowed by the sponge-like effects of water seeping into their clothing. Such protective overgarments as padded jacks and brigandines, studded with metal fastenings, would have caused their owners great problems once soaked with water, and the effects of heavy armour on such a submerged body in this situation is self-evident. Many unfortunate Lancastrians must have been drowned by just this problem in the push and shove to reach the opposite bank, not forgetting of course that the Yorkists were killing many and relentlessly hounding their speed of retreat in the process to make matters even worse. Edward Hall gives his lasting impression of the rout from the field of battle when the Lancastrians,

> like men amazed, fled towards Tadcaster bridge to save themselves, but in the mean way there was a little brook called Cock, not very broad but of great deepness, in the which, what for haste of escaping, and what for fear of followers, a great number were drent and drowned, in so much that the common people there affirm that men alive passed the river upon the dead carcasses, and that the great river of Wharfe, which is the great sewer of the brook, and of all the water coming from Towton, was coloured with blood.[32]

By late afternoon the whole scene of death and destruction by water and steel must have been horrific. As the rout moved across the blood-soaked banks of the River Cock, the fortunate Lancastrians who had made good their escape early on, and the ones who had managed to cross the river over the bodies of the fallen, raced for Tadcaster across open country to the bridge there. However, much the same manner of death awaited the Lancastrians here as one misfortune after another caused the battle of Towton's casualty list to rise further as men drowned trying to cross the River Wharfe or were speared to death near its bridge and in the streets of Tadcaster.

The rout was utter and complete, leaving Lancastrian corpses all across the countryside. However, the battlefield itself must have been a far worse place to behold with such sights as human dams choked with corpses up and down the course of the River Cock and more isolated bodies littering the slopes from the battlefield. On the plateau itself would have been a great expanse of scattered corpses leading to thick tangled heaps of dead in Towton Dale, Bloody Meadow and the battlefield depression, and the telltale snow-covered mounds of the fighting earlier in the day would have been all too apparent. The whole battlefield in the areas of greatest slaughter must have been wholly soaked in blood, on which the jubilant Yorkists now began stripping the dead of their valuables, quickly despatching any Lancastrians who were still alive.

Heralds and their scribes from both sides would have been at work too, counting and recording the dead and making notes of nobles' titles through their coats of arms and badges, so as to distinguish who was next in line, or which titles were vacant to fill. These men would also later have organized the burial parties to begin the inevitable laborious task ahead, once some form of normality returned to the area.

According to the Croyland chronicler it is recorded that King Edward remained on the battlefield of Towton with most of his army while some of his force pursued the Lancastrians, and this is hardly surprising considering the great trial of strength that had been endured by both sides during the day. Many Yorkist knights were created by King Edward after the battle, and it is most likely some of these men were dubbed on the field, while waiting in line to congratulate the new Yorkist monarch may have been a deputation of Lancastrian heralds of arms to beg him for God's mercy for the souls of the dead who had rebelled against him.

Finally, as Palm Sunday drew to a close and darkness enveloped the plateau, the lists of the dead were brought to the king and were read by the light of fires that were once more lit around the village of Towton. This time the victorious Yorkists occupied the village, having beforehand undoubtedly secured much needed supplies from the abandoned Lancastrian baggage park. Here the army's surgeons would have been hard at work too, stitching and cauterizing wounds with their primitive instruments in less than adequate conditions. This would not have been enough in most cases, as infection would in the end claim many wounded in the days to come, and a slow death would ultimately follow fever and disease. For the dying on the field, such a grim form of extinction is hard to contemplate, or indeed attempt to visualize without any amount of human compassion for the sufferers. Exposure on the cold battlefield would eventually have claimed them all as they weakly called for help into the darkness, until the extreme drop in temperature during the early hours finally finished them off.

Amid these scenes of utter destruction and confusion, it became increasingly obvious that an even greater uncertainty threatened the Yorkist regime as night closed in. King Edward for one must have wondered what he had in fact achieved, who had managed to escape the field and whether the haphazard lists of Lancastrian dead were in fact correct or complete. He knew he had won a great battle and that the enemy were completely routed, but as he bent in silent vigil that night to thank God for his victory, many of his advisors' words of congratulation must have fallen on hollow ground as the bodies of such nobles as Somerset, Northumberland, Exeter, Devon and Wiltshire, his mortal enemies, rose yet again to threaten his throne, as none of their bodies had been found on Palmsunday Field.

SEVEN

Nowe ys Thus

W hat happened to the Lancastrian peerage during and after the bloody and complete rout from the battlefield of Towton? At what point did the nobles decide to quit the field, and how did they manage to escape back to York so quickly?

Apart from the erroneous lists of the dead given by chroniclers, who in fact recorded the slain in the whole Towton campaign, a few scraps of evidence do emerge that enable us to piece together the main Lancastrian leaders' whereabouts after the battle. For instance, Gregory's Chronicle maintains that:

> The Earl of Devon was sick [in York], and could not get away, and was taken and beheaded. And the Earl of Wiltshire was taken and brought unto Newcastle to the king. And there his head was smote off and sent unto London to be set upon London Bridge.[1]

Wiltshire's capture at Cockermouth in Cumberland, and his subsequent execution at Newcastle by King Edward, are of course much later events. His capture occurred when the Yorkists had pursued the Lancastrian fugitives further north, and after King Henry, the queen and the Prince of Wales had quit York and had reached Berwick (then in Scotland) safely. The Earl of Wiltshire was quite an expert at extracting himself from very difficult situations. Earlier in the Wars of the Roses at the first battle of St Albans, according to William Gregory, 'this said James [Butler] set the king's banner against a house end and fought manly with his heels, for he was afraid of losing his beauty, for he was named the fairest knight of this land'.[2] Because of this consistent track record of escape from battlefields, it is very likely that the earl was the first to get out of the mêlée at Towton, but he certainly was not alone on this occasion, because the dukes of Somerset and Exeter, Lord Roos and others must have been similarly calling for their horses when the Lancastrian flank was turned in North Acres. They certainly would not have escaped the Yorkist cavalry if they had left it any later than this, and if they had, surely in attempting to run back to their horses in full armour they would have been cut down in the general rout.

According to the Brut Chronicle, after hearing of their defeat at Towton, the Lancastrian royal family fled from York at midnight accompanied by the Duke of Somerset, Lord Roos and others. King Edward arrived in the city with his army the next day (Monday 30 March), and it was here that the 'sick' Earl of Devon and three others, according to Edward Hall, were promptly executed. Their heads replaced the decomposing skulls of the Yorkist nobles executed after the battle of Wakefield three months earlier. The Yorkists were certainly in a vindictive mood even though they had found Lord Montagu and Lord Berners alive and well in the city. They had been captured by the Lancastrians after the second battle of St Albans and had apparently been set free as Edward's army approached Micklegate. This gesture, however, failed to move the king, and he immediately set about rooting out the last pockets of Lancastrian resistance in the area.

As regards the whereabouts of other Lancastrian nobles, some authorities state that the Earl of Northumberland perished on the battlefield of Towton itself and was found among the dead. He was certainly wounded, but may have reached York with the rest of the nobility, only to die from his injuries later in the day. He was buried in the church of St Denis in Walmgate, York, 'In the north choir under a large blue marble stone, which had two effigies on it and an inscription in brass around it'.[3] Unfortunately in 1736 this tomb was obliterated and only the tradition remains, although St Denis was the parish church of the Percy family and opposite once stood the palace of the earls of Northumberland.

The city of York was, without doubt, the Lancastrian nobles' destination after their flight from the battle of Towton, not only to warn the king to flee, but also because this was their own best escape route north into Scotland. The small contingent of gentry, their servants and some of their household would probably have left their confused battle-line at Towton in command of the army's most able knights, as the Duke of Norfolk's forces began to press the Lancastrian flank. Certainly such courageous men as Lord Dacre, Lord Welles, Lord Willoughby, Lord Mauley and many other lesser knights and squires were left dead on the field of battle, including Sir Andrew Trollope. They may not even have seen Somerset and the others depart, and some of them may already have been killed in action as their leaders splashed across the ford that would soon become one of the infamous bridges of bodies across the River Cock.

En route to York at Tadcaster the Duke of Somerset may have ordered the bridge over the River Wharfe to be broken down to delay the enemy and protect King Henry, aware that, if he did not, the pursuing Yorkist cavalry would soon reach York and capture them all as they endeavoured to bundle the Lancasters out of the city. As mentioned earlier, this action at Tadcaster unfortunately caused the last major disaster of the day as the Lancastrian refugees from the battle tried to cross the River Wharfe.

It was here without doubt that the greatest drownings and killing occurred after the battle of Towton. With respect to the Lancastrian casualties in the rout, George Neville's letter to Coppini a few weeks after the engagement places more emphasis on the River Wharfe crossing as being the main culprit for large-scale drownings compared with the River Cock, which he fails to mention. Because of these casualties while attempting to ford such a major obstacle as the Wharfe, we must increase our original death toll on Palm Sunday even further, and also claim a near annihilation of that part of the Lancastrian army that tried to cross there.

It seems to me obvious that there was, and consequently always has been, some degree of confusion among historians surrounding the two rivers linked with the battle of Towton. In particular, the unsupported claims of the River Cock being 'in spate' on Palm Sunday have certainly been badly misinterpreted, probably to account for the unusually high death tolls in such a small river. Admittedly the River Cock did claim many lives, and ran red with blood because of the slaughter across it, but the Wharfe is, and was then, a much more formidable obstacle, and consequently must account for the greater casualties compared with its small tributary, which was, in Edward Hall's words, only a brook.

Undoubtedly many escaped the battle of Towton in different directions, because Edward IV's attainder document lists many who are not labelled as 'late' (denoting their deaths) before their title. However, on the field, many knights and lords were eventually found dead among the debris and taken away by relatives and friends, such as the Lancastrian Lord Welles, who is buried in St Oswalds church at Methley, West Yorkshire, the home of his first wife Joan Waterton. A fine alabaster tomb, and an even more remarkable likeness of him in typical armour of the period, still exists there in the family's chapel.

On Monday 30 March, King Edward left Towton for York with his victorious Yorkist army. For those left behind with the responsibility of clearing the battlefield and digging the graves of the slain, it was immediately apparent that an unprecedented task lay ahead considering that the bodies covered such a large area. We may therefore conclude, given the inclement weather, that this operation took a very long time and that the dead were not buried straight away as was usual, principally to prevent the spread of disease. The Croyland chronicler in recording his estimate of casualties at the battle of Towton added another ten thousand to the heralds' figures for good measure, but nevertheless gave unique evidence that the weather probably changed after the battle, indeed that a thaw set in, enabling the gravediggers to complete their task and also to see where the bodies were under the heaps of snow. The following passage may also indicate that the River Cock did indeed flood due to this rise in temperature, but after 29 March. The Croyland chronicler maintains that

> after distributing rewards among such as brought the bodies of the slain and gave them burial, the king hastened to enter the before named city [York]. Those who helped to inter the bodies, piled up in pits and in trenches prepared for the purpose, bear witness that eight and thirty thousand warriors fell on that day, besides those who were drowned in the river before alluded to, whose numbers we have no means of ascertaining. The blood, too, of the slain, mingling with the snow which at this time covered the whole surface of the earth, afterwards ran down in the furrows and ditches along with the melted snow, in a most shocking manner, for a distance of two or three miles.[4]

Of the named Lancastrian dead, by far the greatest number were squires, yeomen and commoners, including men from all walks of life such as grocers, priests, merchants, clerks, grooms and gentlemen. Also mentioned in King Edward's Act of Attainder are the knights who were killed on Palmsunday Field, although it is not immediately apparent whether or not all of them perished, because some of the presumed dead appear later in records of the wars to complicate matters. William Gregory recorded that forty-two knights were executed after the battle of Towton in the reprisals, which, if nothing else, illustrates King Edward's ruthless bid to consolidate his position and also shows his own unstinting attempt to destroy his enemies' will and ability to oppose him. More important, however, is that, even though many of the gentry had been killed in battle or executed after it, the Lancastrian king and the Duke of Somerset had escaped the clutches of the Yorkists to breath yet again, and also to canvass support farther north and on the continent. Therefore we must admit that the battle of Towton was not as decisive as some would suggest in this respect. We may agree that on the day the Yorkists thoroughly destroyed the Lancastrian 'northern army' in the heart of their own power base, causing carnage and slaughter on an unprecedented scale, but herein lies a deeper meaning that cannot be ignored: no matter how many branches were hewn from the symbolic Wars of the Roses heraldic tree, the trunk and indeed the roots of the title in question still remained intact so long as sons, brothers and the female line survived to threaten again the aggressor. This was true no matter how many commoners suffered during the systematic pruning, and was similarly apparent when the monarch planted new seeds when the tree ceased to exist.

This was the legacy of the Wars of the Roses, when, even after such a decisive victory as that of the battle of Towton, the victor could only temporarily alleviate his problems. To be absolutely sure of power the king in question had to destroy utterly all of the opposing nobles or woo them to his cause. This was not always possible, which is why such important titles as Somerset and Northumberland succeeded to the next in line, who would undoubtedly be by then similarly vindictive and unamenable to any kind of compromise from their families' killers. Consequently, if the title was powerful and the noble very strong-willed, the wars and the quest for consolidation would continue.

With all of this Lancastrian power on the run and its threats of reincarnation a stark reality, King Edward soon put plans into action to capture his enemies. The Bishop of Elpin stated in his letter to Coppini that the king 'sent a great number of men at arms in pursuit of the fugitives, so that not one may escape when taken'.[5] The urgency and importance of this mission is further underlined because news reached London that twenty thousand of Edward's men had been sent from York in pursuit of the Lancastrians and that Newcastle was already besieged. Here King Edward left the Earl of Warwick, Lord Fauconberg and Lord Montagu in command of the army. Having reached as far north as he dared without additional support, the king returned to York where he spent Easter. Gregory's

Chronicle brings to a close this chapter of the Wars of the Roses and the aftermath of the battle of Towton:

And the king tarried in the north a great while and made great inquiries of the rebellions against his father, and took down his father's head from the walls of York, and made all the country [Yorkshire] to be sworn unto him and his laws. And then he returned to London again and there he made 18 knights and many lords, and then he rode to Westminster and there he was crowned the 28th day of June in the year of our Lord 1461, blessed be God of his great grace.[6]

The new king naturally advanced his friends and relatives after his coronation. He made his uncle, Viscount Bouchier, the Earl of Essex, Lord Fauconberg the Earl of Kent, knights, such as Hastings, Wenlock, Herbert, Devereux, Ogle and others, became lords and Edward's younger brother, George, who was later to cause him so much trouble, was created Duke of Clarence. However, of all the participants who fought at Palmsunday Field and who received their just rewards, Warwick the Kingmaker may have been the odd one out, because of his already powerful status. He was consequently treated very coolly by his protégé from then on. After all, because Edward was now king, the earl was, to say the least, impotent as far as real kingmaking was concerned, and we may ask ourselves where did the power-hungry Neville now turn to fulfil his ambitious nature. Warwick was certainly not elevated to duke for all of his efforts to place Edward on the throne of England, and for the moment might have been content with being superior over the Percys in the north, now that the Earl of Northumberland was dead. However, his attitude was eventually to change when the Woodville family found King Edward's Achilles' heel in Elizabeth, their most eligible asset, who was to turn the king's head and, more importantly turn Warwick's in the direction of the king's 'false, fleeting and purg'red'[7] brother Clarence and refuel the Wars of the Roses fire once again.

As for the strong-minded king, he was to have his own way, and he secretly married Elizabeth Woodville while Warwick was away negotiating Edward's marriage elsewhere. Elizabeth became Queen of England in 1464. She was previously Elizabeth Grey, who had been married to Sir John Grey of Groby, allegedly 'slain at York field' (Towton) according to some chronicles, but in fact killed at the second battle of St Albans. She was also the daughter of Lord Rivers, who, with his son, Anthony Woodville, had fought at the battle of Towton in the Duke of Somerset's army. All of these Greys and Woodvilles were staunch Lancastrians, so we may wonder at King Edward's reasoning. After all, were these not his mortal enemies? Nevertheless his infatuation with Elizabeth Woodville eventually helped all of the queen's family to climb the social ladder, after their Lancastrian attainders were reversed in July 1461. Such were the Wars of the Roses. The sponging Woodvilles were later not only to cause Warwick's disaffection from the king, which would ultimately lead to the earl's death at the battle of Barnet in 1471, but also to create further problems for Richard, Duke of Gloucester, Edward's youngest brother, later Richard III, in his attempt to secure the throne for himself in the 1480s.

At the other end of the social scale, what of the humbler soldiers of Palmsunday Field who had come through the battlefield slaughterhouse with as much fateful help as strength and fortitude in war? Many would certainly fight again in the castle sieges and skirmishes in Northumberland, and perhaps, ten years later, some might have been involved in the campaigns of 1471 with King Edward, Warwick and Queen Margaret at Barnet and Tewkesbury. Most Yorkists were greatly rewarded for their services at Towton, like Ralph Vestynden esquire, King Edward's standard bearer, who was given a £10 annuity for the rest of his life 'for the good, agreeable service which he did unto us'.[8]

The common soldiers would undoubtedly have benefited from looting the battlefield at Towton before the local scavengers plundered the area later at will. All would have secured some memento or souvenir in part payment for their ordeal, be it only weapons and additional armour. Even a pair of new boots would have been greatly prized for all their worth for a soldier on the march. As for the Lancastrians after the battle of Towton, most would have disappeared into the Yorkshire landscape and later back to their homes, or north to rejoin King Henry's cause. Even if they remained in the immediate vicinity – after all, this was Lancastrian country – it is very doubtful that they would have incurred King Edward's wrath. In fact Edward's policy must have been quite the reverse to that of the Lancastrian nobility, of whom he had such a hatred, because here in the Yorkshire area was a valuable pool of levies just waiting to be tapped by Commissions of Array if ever the need arose in the future.

Most Lancastrians, however, would have lost much in the way of belongings in their escape from the battlefield, and also later when some of them were in hiding. Thomas Denys, who fought for the Earl of Warwick at the second battle of St Albans, escaped the rout from the battlefield to write to the Pastons about his ordeal, claiming that 'There lost I £20 worth, horse, harness and money and was hurt in divers places'.[9] It is apparent that he was very lucky to be alive in that he barely escaped the field with the clothes on his back. His horse, very probably being left behind in the Yorkist baggage park, his armour discarded for greater speed and his money lost or possibly used to buy a safe passage from the battle zone. Not only this, but he was wounded as well. In fact most of the letters that exist attesting to the Wars of the Roses soldiers' experience of medieval warfare are very explicit in detailing the personal loss of belongings, and in some cases the individuals' mental and emotional state is also mentioned, reflecting, among other emotions, remorse and nervousness.

As we have explored so far, a great deal could be won or lost on the Wars of the Roses battlefield, and, in the aftermath, mothers were written to and friends sought for help. These are echoes of the experiences of soldiers in similar situations in other eras. In fact reluctance to engage in combat ever again is alluded to, not only because of the great financial loss that might befall such a participant, but also, reading between the lines, the apparent fear and deprivation that could follow such a commitment to one side or the other.

To support this theory is the case of John Paston, a participant in the battle of Barnet, who was almost a complete wreck after his flight from the field in 1471. In his letter home he uses such phrases as 'and I beseech you send money . . . I neither have meat, drink or clothes', and further that he was 'now in my greatest need that ever I was in'.[10] This confirms that his predicament then far outweighed the consequences of the battle itself in some respects. In short, the tone of his letter and others like it reiterates the human experience of battle and of its losers' aftershock in terms of nervousness of being caught, vulnerability to physical and mental deprivation resulting from this and, above all, some soldiers' horror and fear of battle itself may have dissuaded them from ever willingly taking up arms again.

This factor alone quite naturally makes us question the size of Wars of the Roses armies overall, and, coupled with the casualty rate, furthers the possibility of lower estimates of both armies at the battle of Towton than the chronicles would have us believe. However, as indicated, the battle was exceptional in that it took place at the most effective time in the wars in terms of the manpower available to both king and noble.

The aftershock of Palmsunday Field on the Lancastrian cause certainly scattered their power far and wide as many loyal followers fortified the great castles of Northumberland against the Yorkist regime. During a skirmish at Hedgeley Moor, another of the Percys was killed, while valiantly launching himself into the thickest part of the Yorkist battle-line, and on 14 May 1464 the last of the main Towton refugees were hunted down by Lord Montagu at the battle of Hexham, where the Duke of Somerset and Lords Roos and Hungerford were deserted by their common levies and were captured and executed within a matter of days. King Henry again made a lucky escape, but at last the Lancastrian cause crumbled in the north and their strong points fell one by one to the Yorkists. The Lancastrian king was finally captured in July 1465, imprisoned in the Tower of London, and King Edward now sat on a secure throne, at least for the time being, his victory on Palmsunday Field just another memory. The next threat to the king would eventually come from within, from the man who had helped to put him on the throne, and who had commanded with him at his most glorious hour at the battle of Towton – but that is another story.

Legacy of a Battlefield

Over the years, Towton battlefield has remained very much the same as it appeared in 1461. In fact travellers such as John Leland would have been most familiar with the area and indeed with the ground that they trod in the Tudor period, apart from the hurtling traffic rushing past Lead on the B1217. As time has passed, some relics of the engagement have been turned up on the field and in the River Cock to attest to this bloody encounter. However, taking into account the battle's size and casualties, very little has been found considering the number of years that the land has been worked and the time people have spent hunting for artifacts on the site.

Today the land is combed by the metal detector, but still the battlefield has yielded little to the owners of these sophisticated sensors, the consensus of opinion being that maybe the most elusive and significant finds have yet to be uncovered beneath the soil. However, it should be argued here that, after such a battle, most of the soldiers' valuables, armour and weapons would have been meticulously searched for and looted as the corpses were systematically stripped naked and thrown into the trenches prepared for them. The cold weather would have aided the looting considerably, and, although we may wonder at the prizes just waiting to be uncovered in the grave mounds of Towton battlefield, once unearthed and exposed to twentieth-century eyes these tumuli may only reveal a sad, tangled mass of bones, prematurely cut down in the most violent and basic way imaginable. Why anyone would want to unearth and remove this sort of find or conduct this form of graverobbing is beyond my reasoning. Preservation of the burial mounds is far more appropriate.

Apart from this, however, some quite significant finds have been collected over the years from Towton battlefield. Some have been deposited in museums and other public repositories, others have been lost, and there are yet others that may not belong to the battle at all. In about 1786 a gold ring weighing an ounce was deposited with the Society of Antiquaries in London and was then placed in the British Museum. The ring is thought to have belonged to the Earl of Northumberland because of a lion passant crest on its face, and many historians believe that this may have been lost by him on the battlefield of Towton. However, the lion rampant is also associated with the Percys in their heraldic achievements, so it could have belonged to a number of nobles who had this common badge. The ring bears no stone, but the inscription around the left-hand half of its circular face is very intriguing and reads 'Nowe ys Thus'. More a personal disclaimer rather than a family motto, in my opinion the words allude to the owner's authority and his signet of power, or perhaps his irreversible seal of approval and benevolence to ones who owed him allegiance. The Percy motto '*Esperance en Dieu*' would have been an obvious feature on the ring if it had belonged to the Northumberland family, and thus the phrase 'Nowe ys Thus' continues to remain a mystery.

Another ring, of silver and gilt with two hands conjoined, was found 'on the field' and was in the possession of Dr Whittaker in 1816, but now its whereabouts are unknown. A rowel spur of brass and gilt with an ornamental scroll pattern was discovered in about 1792 and was given to the Society of Antiquaries of London. An inscription on the shanks reads '*en loial amour, tout mon coer*' ('all my heart in loyal love'). The Towton Dog Collar is also a very interesting and indeed a remarkable find (see Appendix 3), but again this artifact has been lost to a private collector and therefore cannot be authenticated.

Of the weapons and parts of weapons that have been found on the battlefield, by far the most famous is a small 'battle axe' recovered from the River Cock valley, and once owned by the miller at Saxton. It was purchased from him by Colonel Grant, RA, and was preserved in his family until 1854, when it was presented to the Duke of Northumberland, and it has been on show in Alnwick Castle ever since. The axe still bares a handle, although not its original, and is made of oak, measuring 2½ in in the grip. The blade and the handle together measure 18 in long and it is most likely that this weapon was a longbowman's side-arm rather than a knightly killing tool, because of its small size.

A dagger, or 'short sword', was in the possession of the Reverend William Joseph Newman of Badsworth in the Victorian era, but again its whereabouts today are unknown. According to the antiquaries it measured 2 ft 4½ in, including the tang, which was originally inserted into a handle and is comparable to a stiletto dagger, although it is perhaps too long for this type of weapon (most of which measured between 12 and 14 in). It is reputed to have been very narrow, but thick and angular, and at its broadest point was ½ inch wide, which suggests that it was much more like part of a 'smallsword', or 'town' or 'walking sword', of the late seventeenth and early eighteenth centuries than a relic of the battle of Towton.

A spearhead (or pikehead?) was said to have been found on the battlefield and surfaced in the local blacksmith's shop in the 1840s. An 'unknown gentleman' is said to have bought it about this time and then it disappeared, but as regards this elusive artifact and the latter dagger we must regard both as being of very doubtful authenticity indeed. As explained earlier, so-called archaeological finds are very much dependent on the eye of the beholder, especially if they are in a private collection, and as such some of the artifacts turned up on Towton field, or any other battlefield for that matter, can be made to represent almost anything if a piece of the puzzle is missing. It is much more probable in such a case that the finder has uncovered a piece of rusted twentieth-century agricultural equipment rather than the bodkin arrow-head that killed Lord Dacre in 1461.

Of the more mortal remains, in April 1993 a human skull found on the battlefield was deposited with Tadcaster police and underwent forensic tests at York District Hospital. It was found to be of a nineteen-year-old male, dated 1461, and obviously belonged to an individual who took part in the battle of Towton because injuries were sustained to one side of the face, in particular the eye socket. This horrific wound was thought to have been inflicted by a heavy blow on that side of the skull, probably with a poleaxe or similar shafted weapon, which reminds us of just how some of the soldiers in the battle were brutally killed.

With the land being under the plough for so many years, and so little of the finds not being available for viewing, it is awe-inspiring when, occasionally, one can witness with one's own eyes something very special found on Palmsunday Field. It can make one feel quite insignificant in relation to the artifact balanced on the palm of someone's hand. Over the last few years, items unearthed by owners of metal detectors have been coaxed into the light, and also into the public eye, bringing the battle once more to life and causing endless debate among enthusiasts. In the main, the items found on the battlefield site include pieces of armour a few inches wide, buckles, pieces of spur, sword pommel heads, large rivets identified as being from sallets, horse trappings, small samples of chainmail and even a short bodkin arrowhead has surfaced.

Among the more poignant finds, in my view, are the heraldic buttons, some of which display the allegiance of the individual who once owned them. They are all of a similar round shape and size – 20 mm in diameter at the most – and some have broken fixtures in the centre of the back face. However, cast into the metal disc or dome on the front are splendid embellishments of roses and heraldic signs. Buttons with simple cartwheels or Catherine wheels have also been found, and these may have belonged to retainers of such Yorkist knights as Sir John Scott of Ashford, Kent or Sir Humphrey Stafford, proving the existence of these contingents on the field. Engraved buttons bearing Plantagenet emblems have also surfaced on the field of battle.

It is these more personal artifacts from Towton battlefield that bridge the centuries far more vividly for me than any of the other finds, if only because they are obviously genuine articles from the battle itself and not part of, or belonging to, a missing item. They say so much about what we have been dealing with all along in this book – quite simply the struggle of an individual to survive, or to perish, in such a terrible ordeal out of loyalty, and, more important, the ability of man to conquer fear itself in the worst possible situation imaginable.

There can be no substitute in the experience of battle, medieval or otherwise, for the unfolding of the most basic instincts known to man, and, in particular, of human survival against overwhelming odds. To kill or be killed is a terrible and threatening predicament even to contemplate, let alone to describe or try to account for its morality, when one type of violence or another is an ongoing fact of everyday life. Turn on the television and it is there being described in all of its horror and brutality by those involved in or party to it. However, even in the worst 'last stand' situations, man has triumphed while the greatest of tragedies were played out all around him, performing feats of heroism in the process, in some cases defying all human logic to survive, and finally emerging to tell the story to others in the confines of a secure armchair years later. Some individuals were not so lucky, however, and were inevitably killed in battle, and it is to them that this book is dedicated, mainly because the battle of Towton is not unique, and is only one among hundreds of others inherent, it seems, in man's history and make-up. In short, a matter of respect for the soldiers who fought and died in such battles and wars lies at the heart of the events described here, and as such we must always honour that standard.

Towton battlefield is one of the few remaining sites that retains its historical identity, and, apart from cultivation, the land and the battle's unique places of interest are still intact over five hundred years later in a fifteenth-century time capsule, just waiting to be experienced. Let's hope it stays like that.

Appendices

I   King Edward IV's Act of Attainder

The following is an extract from King Edward IV's Act of Attainder, passed against the Lancastrians after the battle of Towton. It is useful in so much as it contains some of the names of those who fought for King Henry VI on Palm Sunday, 29 March 1461.

And where also Henry Duke of Exeter, Henry Duke of Somerset, Thomas Courtenay, late Earl of Devonshire, Henry, late Earl of Northumberland, William Viscount Beaumont, Thomas Lord Roos, John, late Lord Clifford, Leo, late Lord Welles, John, late Lord Neville, Thomas Grey Knight, Lord Rugemond-Grey, Randolf, late Lord Dacre, Humphrey Dacre Knight, John Morton, late Person of Blokesworth in the shire of Dorset Clerk, Rauf Makerell, late Person of Ryseby, in the shire of Suffolk Clerk, Thomas Manning, late of New Windsor in Berkshire Clerk, John Whelpdale, late of Lichfield in the county of Stafford Clerk, John Nayler, late of London Squire, John Preston, late of Wakefield in the shire of York Priest, Philip Wentworth Knight, John Fortescue Knight, William Tailboys Knight, Edmund Moundford Knight, Thomas Tresham Knight, William Vaux Knight, Edmund Hampden Knight, Thomas Findern Knight, John Courtenay Knight, Henry Lewes Knight, Nicholas Latimer Knight, Walter Nuthill, late of Ryston in Holderness in the shire of York Squire, John Heron of the Forde Knight, Richard Tunstall Knight, Henry Bellingham Knight, Robert Whitingham Knight, John Ormond otherwise called John Butler Knight, William Mille Knight, Simon Hammes Knight, William Holand Knight called the Bastard of Exeter, William Joseph, late of London Squire, Everard Digby, late of Stokedry in the shire of Rutland Squire, John Mirfin of Southwalk in the shire of Surrey Squire, Thomas Philip, late of

Dertington in Devonshire Squire, Thomas Brampton, late of Guines Squire, Giles Saintlowe, late of London Squire, Thomas Claymond, the said Thomas Tunstall Squire, Thomas Crawford, late of Calais Squire, John Audley, late of Guines Squire, John Lenche of Wich in the shire of Worcester Squire, Thomas Ormond otherwise called Thomas Butler Knight, Robert Bellingham, late of Burnalshede in the shire of Westmorland Squire, Thomas Everingham, late of Newhall in the shire of Leicester Knight, John Penycock, late of Waybridge in the county of Surrey Squire, William Grimsby, late of Grimsby in the shire of Lincoln Squire, Henry Ross, late of Rockingham in the shire of Northampton Knight, Thomas Daniel, late of Rising in the shire of Norfolk Squire, John Doubigging, late of the same Gentleman, Richard Kirkby, late of Kirkby Ireleth in the shire of Lancaster Gentleman, William Ackworth, late of Luton in the shire of Bedford Squire, William Weynsford, late of London Squire, Richard Stuckley, late of Lambeth in the county of Surrey Squire, Thomas Stanley, late of Carlisle Gentleman, Thomas Litley, late of London Grocer, John Maidenwell, late of Kirton in Lindsey in the county of Lincoln Gentleman, Edward Ellesmere, late of London Squire, John Dawson, late of Westminster in the shire of Middlesex Yeoman, Henry Spencer, late of the same Yeoman, John Smothing, late of York Yeoman, John Beaumont, late of Goodby in the shire of Leicester Gentleman, Henry Beaumont, late of the same Gentleman, Roger Wharton otherwise called Roger of the Halle, late of Burgh in the shire of Westmorland Groom, John Joskin, late of Branghing in the shire of Hertford Squire, Richard Lister the younger of Wakefield Yeoman, Thomas Carr, late of Westminster Yeoman, Robert Bolling, late of Bolling in the shire of York Gentleman, Robert Hatecale, late of Barleburgh in the same shire Yeoman, Richard Everingham, late of Pontefract in the same shire Squire, Richard Fulnaby of Fulnaby in the shire of Lincoln Gentleman, Laurence Hill, late of Much Wycombe in the county of Buckingham Yeoman, Rauff Chernok, late of Thorley in the county of Lancaster Gentleman, Richard Gaitford of Estretford in Cley in the shire of Nottingham Gentleman, John Chapman, late of Wimbourne Minster in Dorset shire Yeoman, and Richard Cokerell, late of York Merchant; on Sunday called commonly Palm Sunday the 29th day of March the first year of his reign, in a field between the towns of Sherburn-in-Elmet and

Tadcaster, in the said shire of York, called Saxtonfield and Towtonfield, in the shire of York, accompanied with Frenchmen and Scots, the Kings enemies, falsely and traitorously against their faith and liegeance, there reared war against the same King Edward, their rightwise, true, and natural liege lord, purposing there and then to have destroyed him, and deposed him of his royal estate, crown, and dignity, and then and there to that intent, falsely and traitorously moved battle against his said estate, shedding therin the blood of a great number of his subjects. In the which battle it pleased almighty God to give unto him, of the mystery of his might and grace, the victory of his enemies and rebels, and to subdue and avoid the effect of their false and traitorous purpose.

Rot. Parl. 1st Edward IV. 1461, Vol. V fo. 477–8.

2 Sir William Plumpton's Contingent

On 13 March 1461 Sir William Plumpton was summoned by King Henry VI to attend him in York with as many men as possible. The resulting contingent raised by Sir William went into action at Towton, sixteen days later, where Plumpton's eldest son was killed in battle:

To our trusty and welbeloved knight, Sir William Plumpton.

By the King R.H.[1] Trusty and welbeloved, we greet you well, and for as much as we have very knowledge that our great traitor, the late Earl of March,[2] hath made great assemblies of riotous and mischievously disposed people, and to stir and provoke them to draw unto him, he hath cried in his proclamations havoc upon all our true liege people and subjects, their wives, children, and goods, and is now coming towards us, we therefore pray you and also straightly charge you that anon upon the sight hereof, ye, with all such people as ye may make defensible arrayed, come unto us in all haste possible, where so ever we shall be within this our Realm, for to resist the malicious intent and purpose of our said traitor, and fail not hereof as ye love the security of our person, the weal of yourself, and of all our true and faithful subjects. Given under our signet at our City of York, the thirteenth day of March. (1460–61).

Plumpton Letters (ed.) Thomas Stapleton, Camden Society 1839, letter 1.

3   'The Towton Dog Collar'

The following story appeared in the *Yorkshire Evening Post* on 20 April 1926.

£1,500 COLLAR FOUND AT TOWTON BATTLE RELIC; WOMAN
RECALLS PLOUGHMAN'S TREASURE

Mrs. Davis, a widow, now living in Hunslet, took an especial interest in
the story of the battle of Towton because of her birth in Saxton village
where her father, Mr. Edward Warrington, was the village shoemaker and
also clerk and sexton at Saxton Parish Church. He had much to do with
the restoration and proper preservation of Lord Dacre's tomb in the
churchyard. Mrs. Davis is now 69, and we give the story as she tells it.

'I wrote to you about a supposed-to-be brass ring', she said, 'which
was turned up by the plough in one of the fields on Saxton Grange
Farm about 55 years ago. I could go very nearly blind-folded to the
spot now. Mr. Henry Smart had the farm then, and I was a girl of
about 14 working there. Tom Ambler, who came from Church
Fenton, was there as second wagoner. He ploughed this ring up in the
field and said it would make a nice collar for the dog, a black retriever
we had on the farm. I have put the collar on and off many a time. I
called it a ring, but it was quite a big collar. It was all caked up and
clogged, but as we brushed the dirt off it we found that it was made of
moveable parts in such a way that when it was small – closed up like –
it was broad, and as it stretched out it went narrower. It was fastened
with a sort of clasp.

'It was a battle relic right enough. We thought it was just a brass
collar at first and then one day Mr. Benjamin Hey of Sherburn came
shooting with Mr. Smart. They took the retriever with them and
looking at the collar Mr. Hey asked where it came from and then said,
"I'll give you £5 for t'collar Harry."

'Mr. Smart said, "Nay, if its worth £5 to you its worth £5 to me,"
and they began to examine it. The dog had been wearing it about
eight months and it had begun to shine and some things on it that we
took for studs had begun to glitter. They turned out to be gems and
rubies, and what we thought was brass was gold.

'"I'd have it valued Harry," said Mr. Hey, and they took it to York and the man they took it to offered them £600 for it straight away. They sold it and the last we heard of that collar was that it had been sold at one of the sale rooms in London for £1,500. I think it was at that place – you know Christies. And all that Tom Ambler, who ploughed it up, got was two pints of beer. I served him with it out of the barrel in the kitchen.'

Could this collar have been a chain of office worn by a noble at the battle of Towton, or something more ancient perhaps? What makes the story more interesting, and personally ironic, is the fact that I may be related on my paternal grandmother's side of the family to the Tom Ambler of Church Fenton who unearthed it.

Abbreviations

15th-Cent. Chron.	*Three Fifteenth-Century Chronicles*, ed. J. Gairdner
Arrivall	*Historie of the Arrivall of King Edward IV*, ed. J. Bruce
Benet	John Benet, *Chronicle*, eds G.L. Harriss and M.A. Harriss
BP	P. Makin, *Provence and Pound*, Bertrand's Propaganda
Brooke	R. Brooke, *The Field of the Battle of Towton*
Burne	A.H. Burne, *Battlefields of England*
Commynes	Philip de Commynes, *Memoirs*, tr. Michael Jones
Croyland	*Croyland Abbey Chronicle*, ed. H.T. Riley
CSPM	*Calendar of State Papers of Milan*, ed. A.B. Hinds
Davies	*An English Chronicle of the Reigns of Richard II, Henry IV, Henry V and Henry VI*, ed. J.S. Davies
Drake	F. Drake, *Eboracum*
Forrest	C. Forrest, *The History of Knottingley*
Froissart	*Froissart's Chronicles*, ed. G. Brereton
Great Chron.	*The Great Chronicle of London*, eds A.H. Thomas and I.D. Thomas
Gregory	'Gregory's Chronicle' in *The Historical Collections of a Citizen of London*, ed. J. Gairdner
Hall	Edward Hall, *Chronicle*, ed. H. Ellis
Hearne	'Hearne's Fragment' in *Chronicles of the White Rose*, ed. J.A. Giles
Keegan	J. Keegan, *The Face of Battle*
Latimer	*Sermons by Hugh Latimer*, ed. G.E. Corrie
Leland	John Leland, *Itinerary*
Paston	*The Paston Letters*, ed. J. Gairdner
RBN	*Records of the Borough of Nottingham*
Rose of Rouen	'The Rose of Rouen', *Archaeologia* XXIX
Rot. Parl.	*Rotuli Parliamentorum*

Vergil	Polydore Vergil, *English History,* ed. H. Ellis
Waurin	Jean de Waurin, *Recueil des Chroniques d'Engleterre,* eds W. Hardy and E.L.C.P. Hardy
Wheater	W. Wheater, *The History of Sherburn and Cawood*
Whethamstede	*Registrum Abbatis Johannis Whethamstede,* ed. H.T. Riley
Whittaker	R. Whittaker, *Leodis and Elmete*
Worcester	William Worcester, *Annales Rerum Anglicarum,* ed. Stevenson
York Civic Records	*York Civic Records,* ed. A. Raine

Notes

Chapter One

1. *CSPM*, pp. 61–2.
2. *CSPM*, p. 62.
3. *CSPM*, p. 60.
4. *CSPM*, pp. 64–5.
5. *CSPM*, p. 66.
6. *CSPM*, p. 68.
7. *CSPM*, p. 69.
8. *Paston* 3, pp. 267–8.
9. Keegan, pp. 87–8.
10. Shakespeare's Henry V Prologue.
11. *15th-Cent. Chron.*, p. 94.
12. Benet, pp. 206–7.
13. *Paston* 3, p. 13.
14. *Paston* 3, p. 13.
15. Gregory, p. 204.
16. *Whethamstede*, pp. 376–8.
17. *Whethamstede*, pp. 376–8.

Chapter Two

1. *Whethamstede*, pp. 381–2; Waurin, p. 325.
2. Davies, pp. 106–7.
3. Worcester, 2, p. 775.
4. Hall, p. 250.
5. Leland, p. 242.
6. Gregory, p. 208.
7. Davies, pp. 106–7.
8. *Rot. Parl.* 5, pp. 375–9.
9. Worcester, 2, p. 775.
10. Gregory, p. 211.
11. Hall, p. 251.
12. Hall, p. 251.
13. Gregory, p. 211.
14. Gregory, p. 211.
15. *Croyland*, p. 423.
16. Gregory, p. 212.
17. *Whethamstede*, pp. 388–92.
18. Gregory, pp. 213–14.
19. Gregory, p. 212.
20. Gregory, p. 214.
21. Rose of Rouen, pp. 343–7.

Chapter Three

1. Worcester, 2, p. 775.
2. *Great Chron.* pp. 194–6.
3. Worcester, 2, p. 777.
4. Hearne, p. 8.
5. *CSPM*, p. 61.
6. Hearne, pp. 8–9.
7. Rose of Rouen, pp. 343–7.
8. *Paston*, 6, p. 85.
9. *York Civic Records*, 1, p. 135.
10. Gregory, p. 214.

Chapter Four

1. *CSPM*, p. 61.
2. Gregory, p. 216.
3. Hearne, p. 9.
4. Hall, pp. 254–5.
5. Hall, p. 255.
6. Waurin, pp. 337–8.
7. Hall, pp. 254–5.
8. Forrest, pp. 127–8.
9. Forrest, p. 17.
10. Benet, p. 230.
11. Hall, p. 255.

12. Waurin, p. 338.
13. Forrest, p. 105.
14. Forrest, p. 102.
15. Waurin, p. 338.

Chapter Five

1. Leland, pp. 243–4.
2. Brooke, pp. 112–13.
3. Leland, p. 243.
4. Brooke, p. 115.
5. Leland, p. 243.
6. Leland, p. 243.
7. Brooke, p. 123.
8. Wheater, p. 70.
9. Whittaker, p. 156.
10. Leland, p. 243.
11. Brooke, p. 91.
12. Harleian MS795.
13. Whittaker, p. 156.
14. Leland, p. 243.
15. Drake, p. 111.
16. Hall, p. 255.
17. Leland, p. 243.
18. *Rot. Parl.* 5, pp. 477–8.
19. Waurin, pp. 339–40.

Chapter Six

1. Rose of Rouen, pp. 343–7.
2. *CSPM*, p. 62.
3. Burne, p. 105.
4. *Paston*, 3, pp. 267–8.
5. Hall, p. 255.
6. Vergil, p. 222.
7. Vergil, pp. 110–11.
8. Keegan, pp. 113, 326.
9. Latimer, p. 167.
10. Hall, pp. 255–6.
11. Vergil, p. 111.

12. Froissart, pp. 88–9.
13. Commynes, p. 71.
14. Hall, p. 256.
15. Waurin, p. 340.
16. BP, pp. 43–9
17. Vergil, p. 111.
18. *RBN*, 2, p. 377.
19. Vergil, pp. 223–4.
20. Commynes, p. 181
21. *CSPM*, p. 64.
22. Waurin, p. 340.
23. *Arrivall*, pp. 28–30.
24. Hearne, p. 9.
25. *Croyland*, p. 426.
26. *CSPM*, p. 62.
27. *Arrivall*, pp. 20–1.
28. Hearne, p. 9.
29. Vergil, p. 111.
30. Commynes, p. 187.
31. *Croyland*, p. 425.
32. Hall, p. 256.

Chapter Seven

1. Gregory, pp. 217–18.
2. Gregory, p. 198.
3. Drake, p. 306.
4. *Croyland*, p. 425.
5. *CSPM*, p. 66.
6. Gregory, p. 218.
7. Shakespeare's Richard III, Act I, Scene IV.
8. *Rot. Parl.* 5, p. 545.
9. *Paston*, 3, p. 274.
10. *Paston*, 5, p. 102.

Appendix 2

1. Henry VI.
2. Edward IV.

Bibliography

Primary Sources

'John Benet's Chronicle for the years 1400–1462', ed. G.L. Harriss and
    M.A. Harriss in *Camden Miscellany*, 24, 1972

Brut, *The Brut Chronicle*, 2 vols, ed. F.W.D. Brie, 1906

Calender of State Papers and Manuscripts in the Archives and Collections of Milan,
    vol. 1. 1385–1618, ed. A.B. Hinds, 1912

Commynes, Philip de, *The memoirs for the Reign of Louis XI, 1461-1483,* tr.
    Michael Jones, 1972

Croyland Abbey Chronicle, ed. H.T. Riley, 1854

Dorset County Record Office, The Bridport Muster Roll 1457

*An English Chronicle of the Reigns of Richard II, Henry IV, Henry V and Henry
    VI*, ed. J.S. Davies, 1856

Friossart, *Froissart's Chronicles*, ed. G. Brereton, 1968

The Great Chronicle of London, eds A.H. Thomas and I.D. Thomas,
    1939

'Gregory's Chronicle' in *The Historical Collections of a Citizen of London*, ed.
    J. Gairdner, 1876

Hall, Edward, *Chronicle*, ed. H. Ellis, 1809

'Hearne's Fragment' in *Chronicles of the White Rose*, ed. J.A. Giles, 1834

Histoirie of the Arrivall of Edward IV, 1471, ed. J. Bruce, 1838

Latimer, Hugh, *Sermons by Hugh Latimer, Bishop of Worcester, 1555*, ed. G.E.
    Corrie, 1844–5

Leland, J., 'Itinerary, 1558' in *Yorkshire Archaeological and Topographical Journal*,
    10, 1889

The Paston Letters, 1422–1509 A.D., ed. James Gairdner, 3 vols, 1872–5

Plumpton Letters, ed. T. Stapleton, Camden Society, 1839

Records of the Borough of Nottingham, Vol. 2, 1883–5

Registrum Abbatis Johannis Whethamstede, ed. H.T. Riley, 1872

'The Rose of Rouen' in *Archaeologicia*, XXIX, pp. 344–7

Rotuli Parliamentorum, 6 vols, 1767

Three Fifteenth-Century Chronicles, ed. J. Gairdner, Camden Society, 1880

Vergil, Polydore, *Three Books of Polydore Vergil's English History*, ed. H. Ellis, 1844

Waurin, Jean de, *Recueil des Chroniques D'Engleterre*, eds W. Hardy and E.L.C.P. Hardy, 1891

Worcester, William, *Annales Rerum Anglicarum*, ed. Stevenson, 1864

York Civic Records, ed. A. Raine, Yorkshire Archaeological Society, Record Series, 98, 1939

Secondary Sources

Bogg, E., *Lower Wharfedale*, 1904.

Brooke, R., 'The field of the battle of Towton', a paper read before the Society of Antiquaries, 1849.

Brooke, R., *Visits to Fields of Battle in England*, 1857.

Brooke-Little, J.P., *Boutell's Heraldry* (revised edn), 1973.

Burne, A.H., *Battlefields of England*, 1950.

Drake, F., *Eboracum*, 1736.

Dunham, W.H., 'Lord Hasting's Indentured Retainers 1461–1483'. *Transactions of the Connecticut Academy of Arts and Sciences*, Sept. 1955.

Forrest, C., *The History of Knottingley*, 1871.

Gillingham, J., *The Wars of the Roses*, 1981.

Goodman, A., *The Wars of the Roses*, 1981.

Hardy, R., *Longbow*, 1976/1992.

Jacob, E.F., *The 15th Century*, Oxford History of England, 1961.

Keegan, J., *The Face of Battle*, 1976.

Kingsford, C.L., *English Historical Literature in the 15th Century*, 1913.

Lander, J.R., *The Wars of the Roses*, 1965, revised 1990.

Makin, P., *Provence and Pound,* Bertrands Propaganda, 1978.

McGill, P., *Heraldic Banners of the Wars of the Roses*, 1990.

Markham, Sir Clement 'The Battle of Towton', *Yorkshire Archaeological and Topographical Journal*, X, 1889.

Oman, Sir Charles, *The Art of War in the Middle Ages,* Vol. 2, 1924.

Perges, G., 'Army Provisioning, Logistics and Strategy in the Second Half of the 17th Century', *Acta Historica*, 16, 1857.

Pollard, A., 'Percies and Nevilles', *History Today*, Sept 1993.

Smurthwaite, D., *The O.S. Guide to the Battlefields of Britain*, 1984.

Storey, R.L., *The End of the House of Lancaster*, 1966.

Wheater, W., *The History of Sherburn and Cawood*, 1865.

Whittaker, R., *Leodis and Elmete*, 1816.

Index